MW01615949

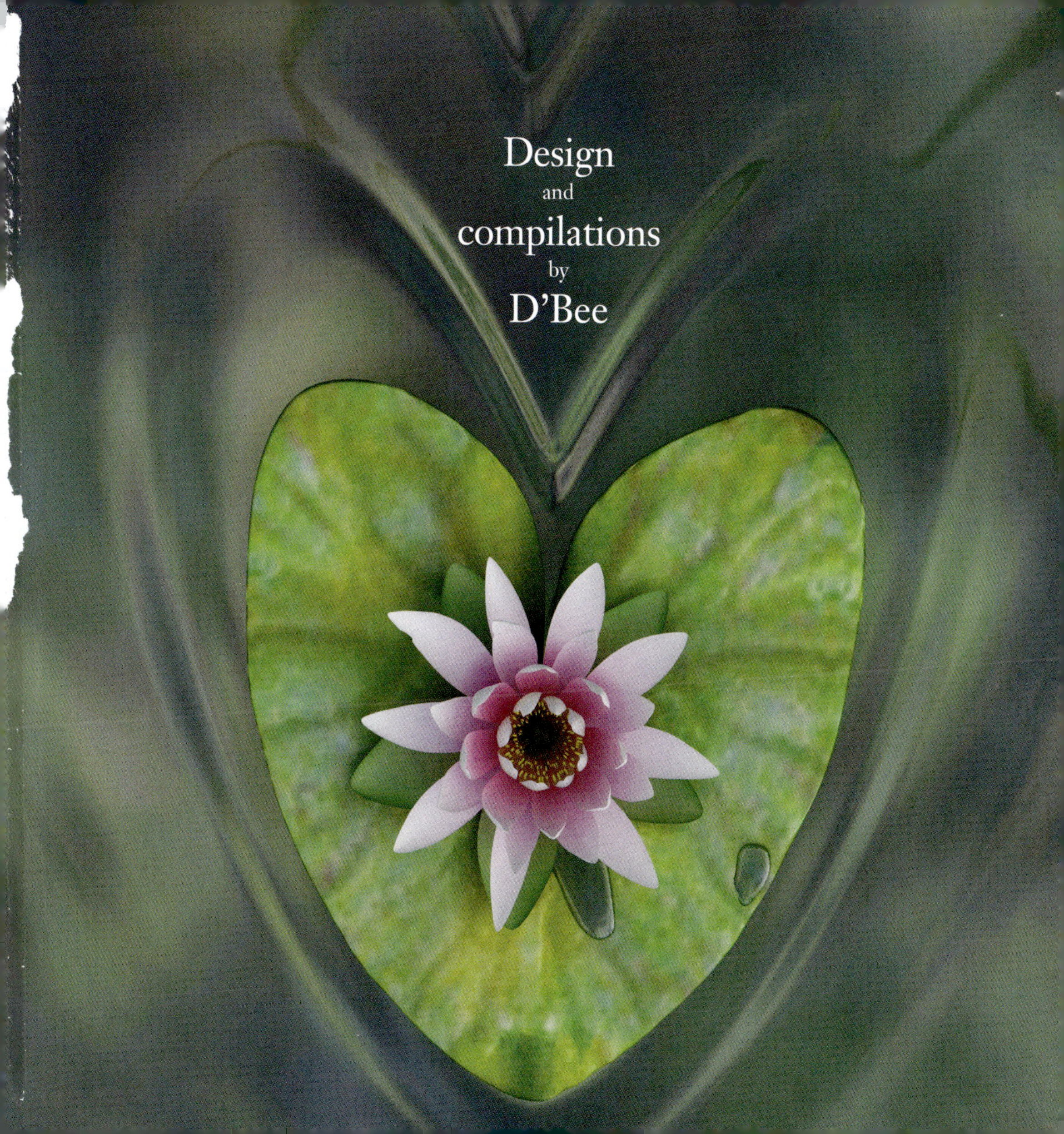

Design
and
compilations
by
D'Bee

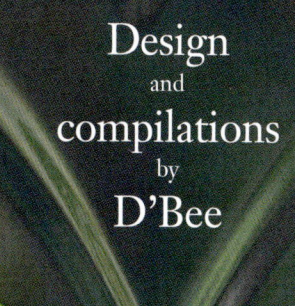

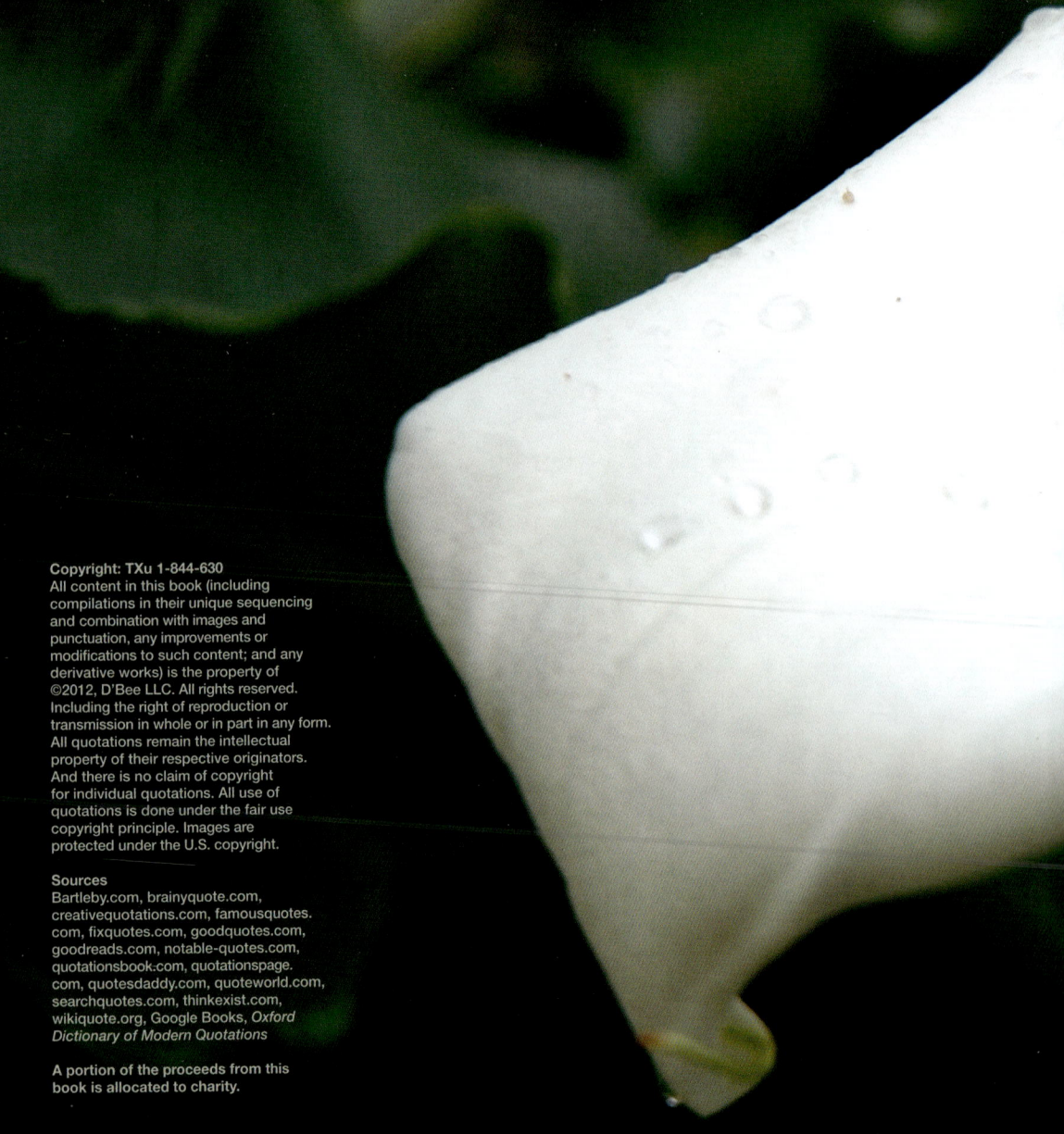

Sources
Bartleby.com, brainyquote.com,
creativequotations.com, famousquotes.
com, fixquotes.com, goodquotes.com,
goodreads.com, notable-quotes.com,
quotationsbook.com, quotationspage.
com, quotesdaddy.com, quoteworld.com,
searchquotes.com, thinkexist.com,
wikiquote.org, Google Books, *Oxford
Dictionary of Modern Quotations*

A portion of the proceeds from this
book is allocated to charity.

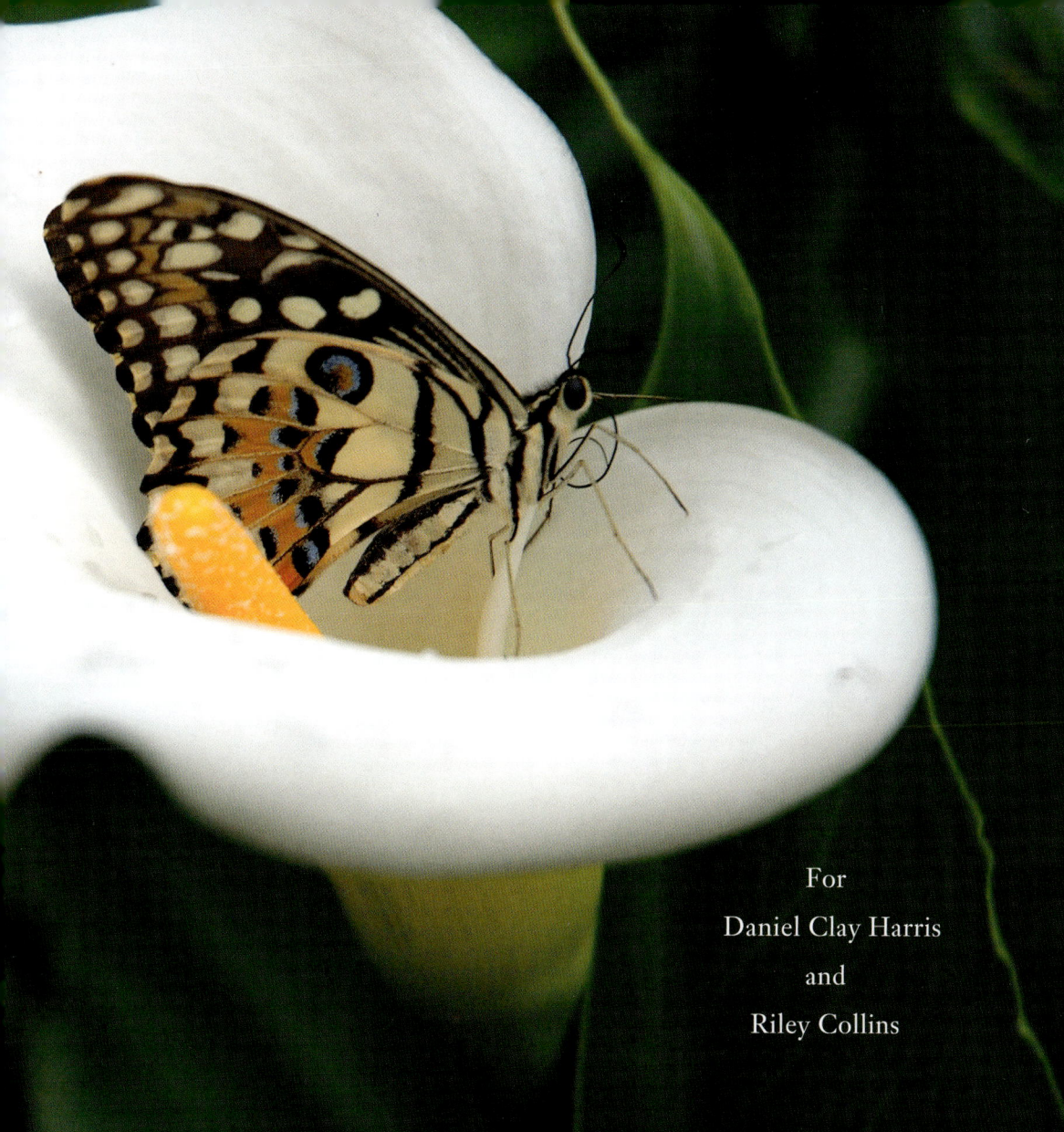

For
Daniel Clay Harris
and
Riley Collins

Nature will bear the closest inspection.

She invites us to lay our eye level

with her smallest leaf,

and take an insect view of its plain.

Henry David Thoreau

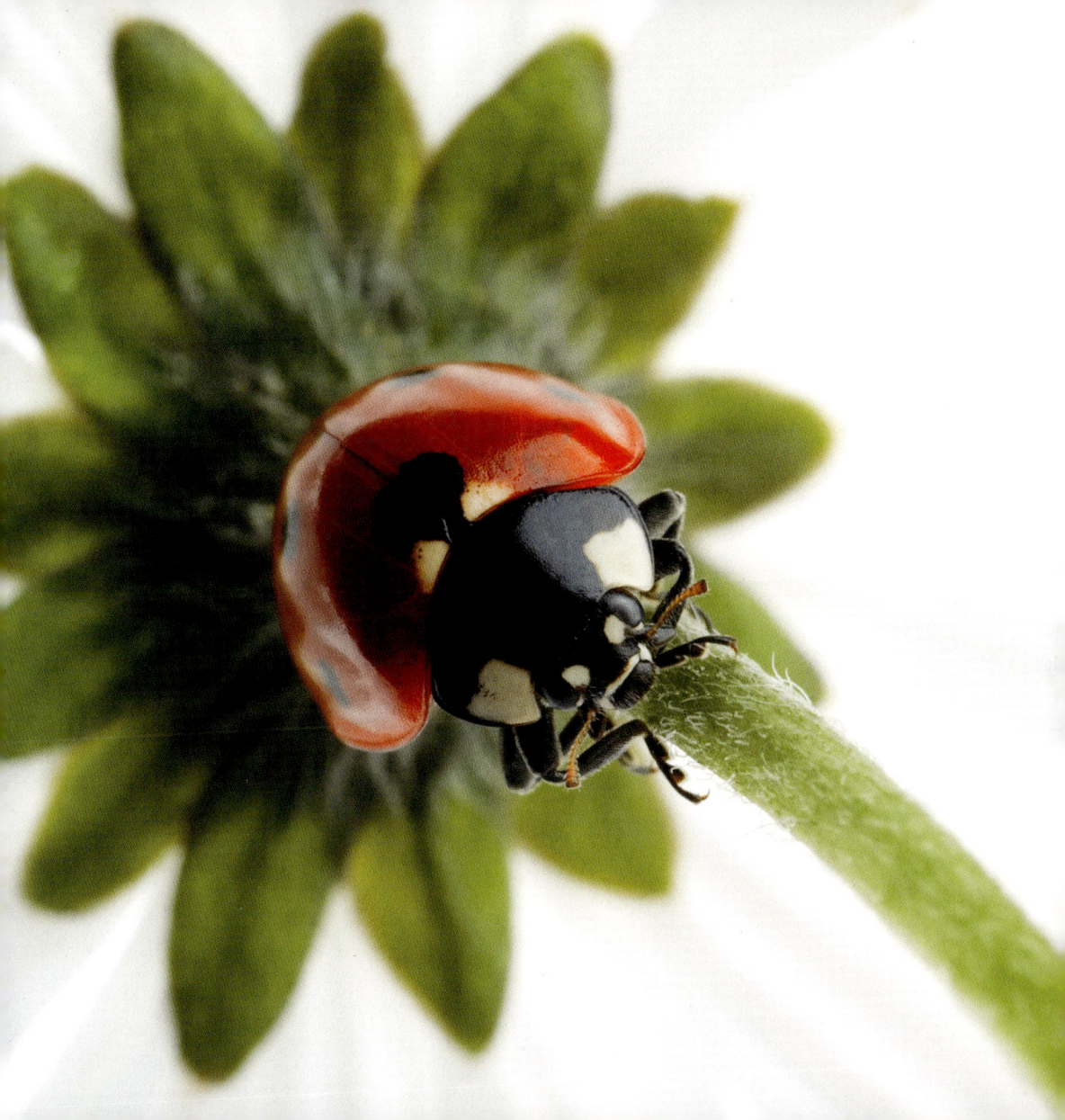

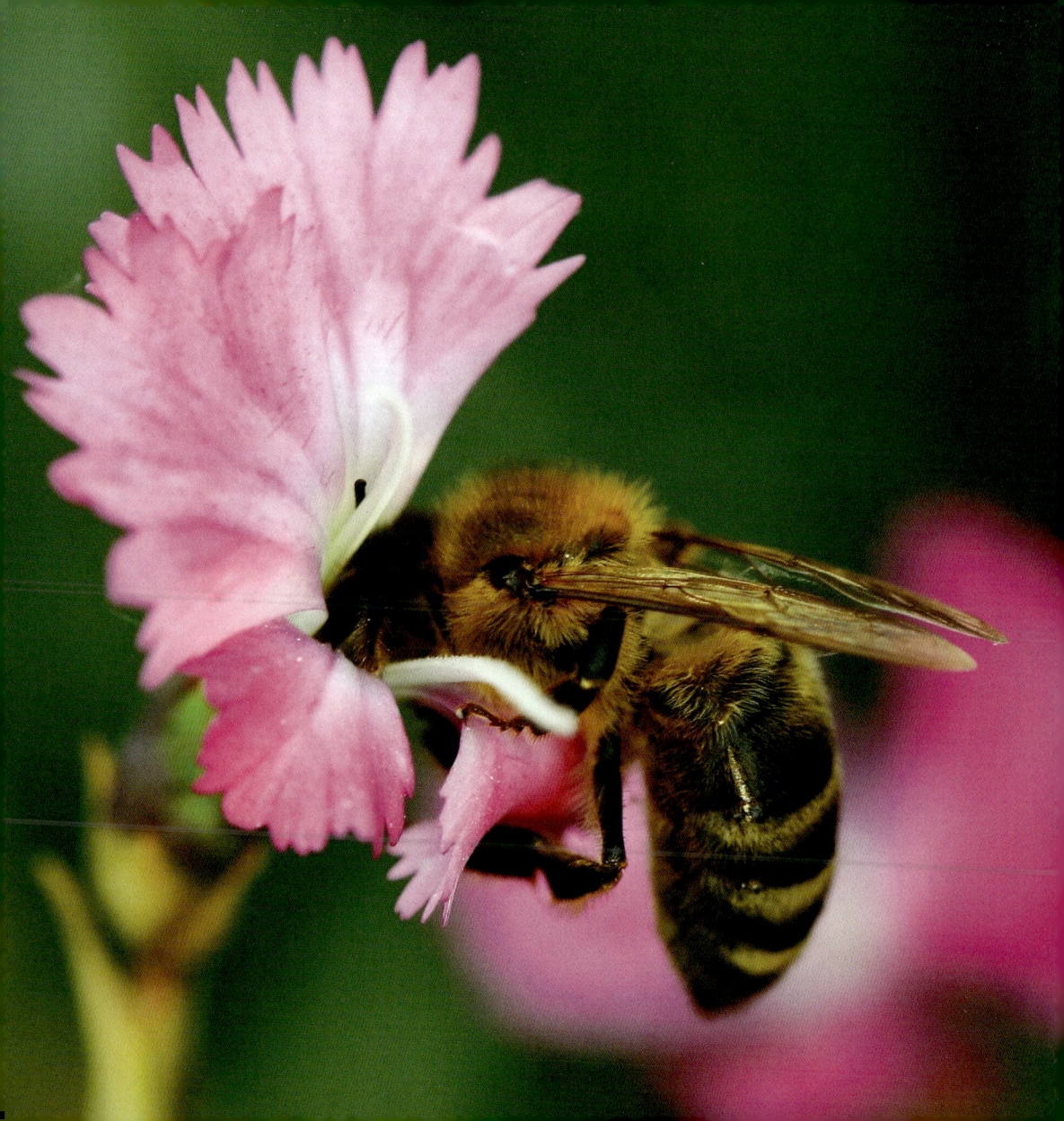

Books are the bees

which carry

the quickening pollen

from one

to another mind.

James Russell Lowell

Poetry is the art of

creating imaginary gardens with real toads.

Marianne Moore

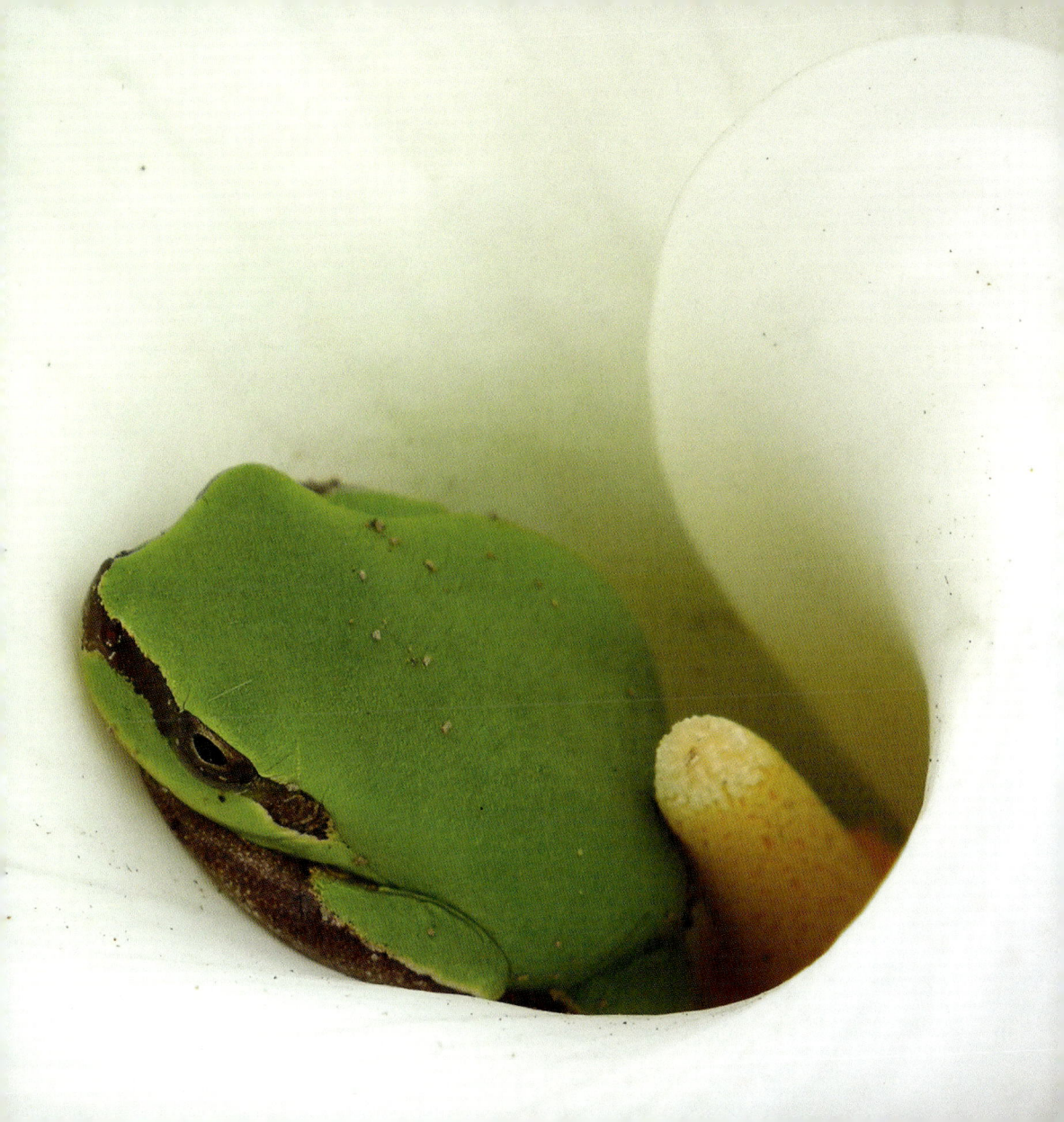

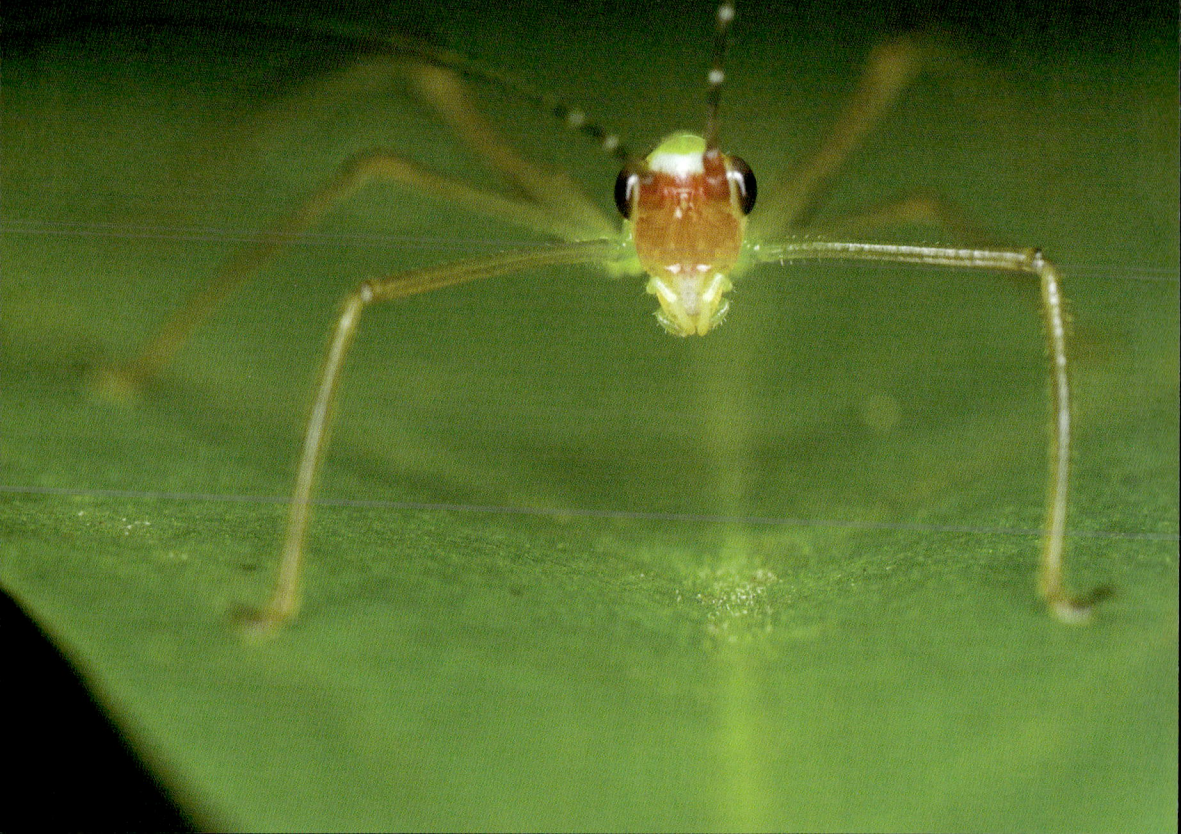

Even larks

and

katydids

are supposed, by some,

to dream.

Shirley Jackson

I believe a leaf of grass

is no less than

the journeywork of the stars.

Walt Whitman

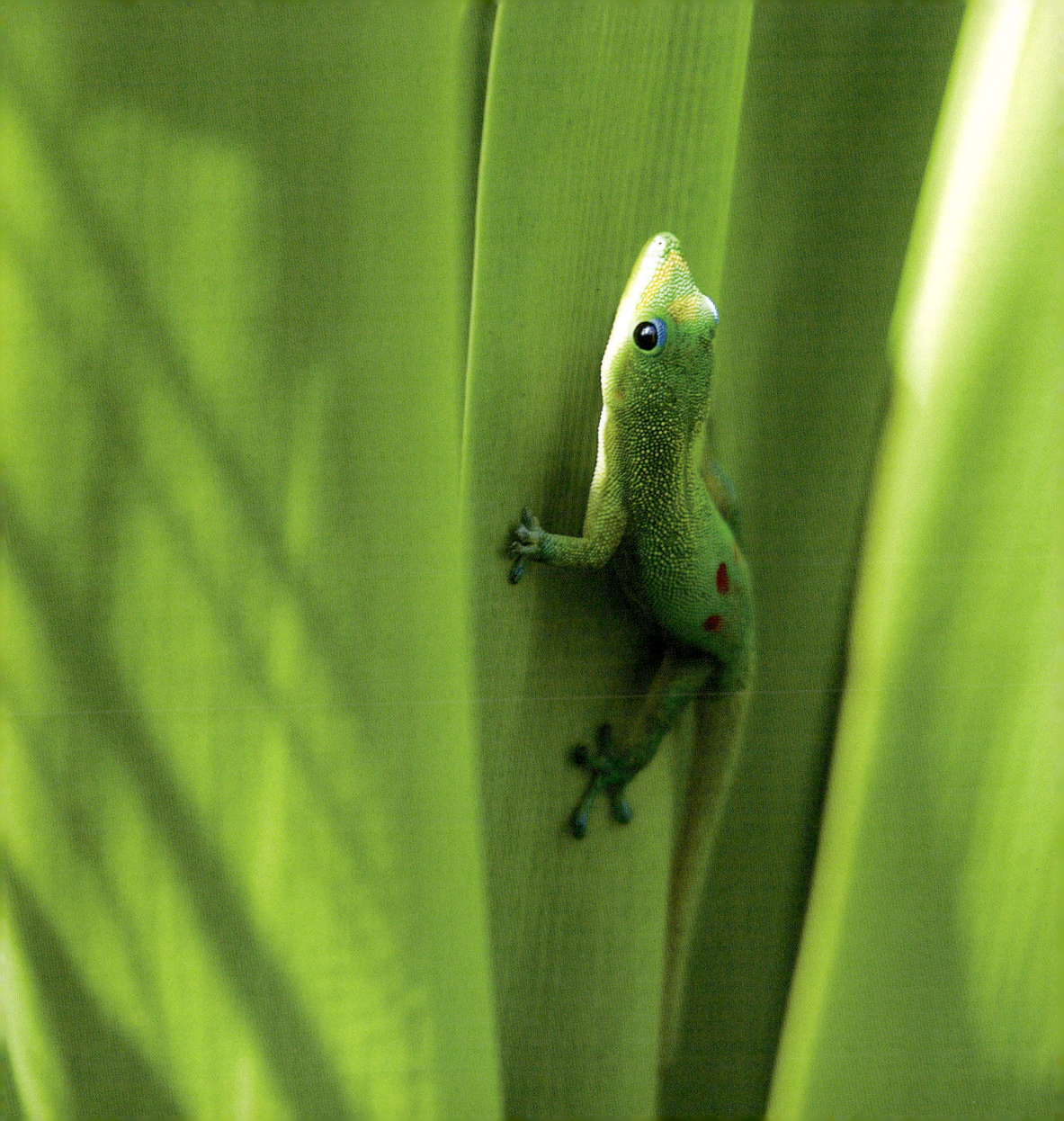

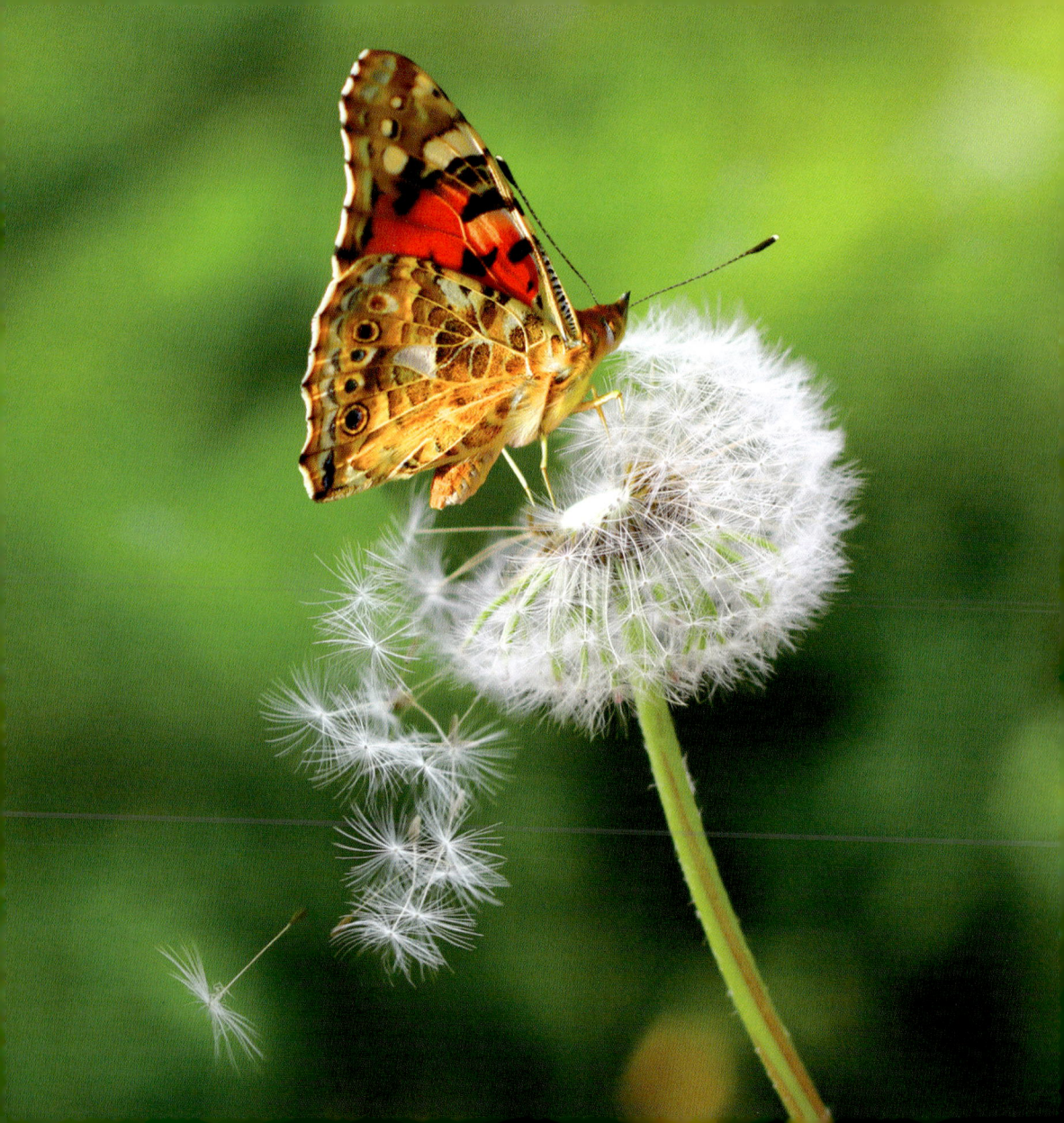

Great things
are done
by a series of
small things
brought together.

Vincent Van Gogh

Depend on

the rabbit's foot if you will,

but remember

it didn't work for the rabbit.

R.E. Shay

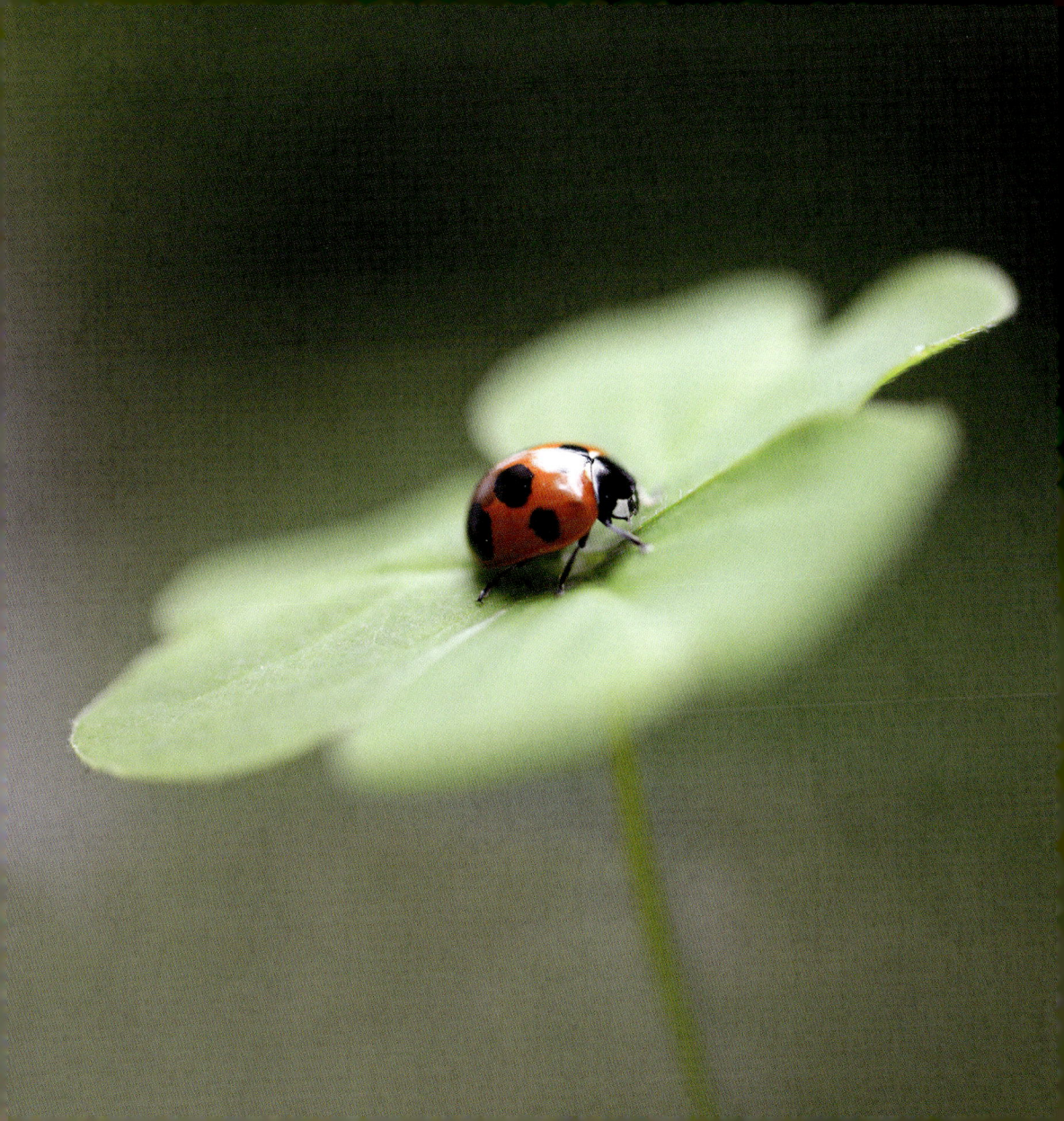

Take time to smell the roses

and eventually

you'll inhale a bee.

Author Unknown

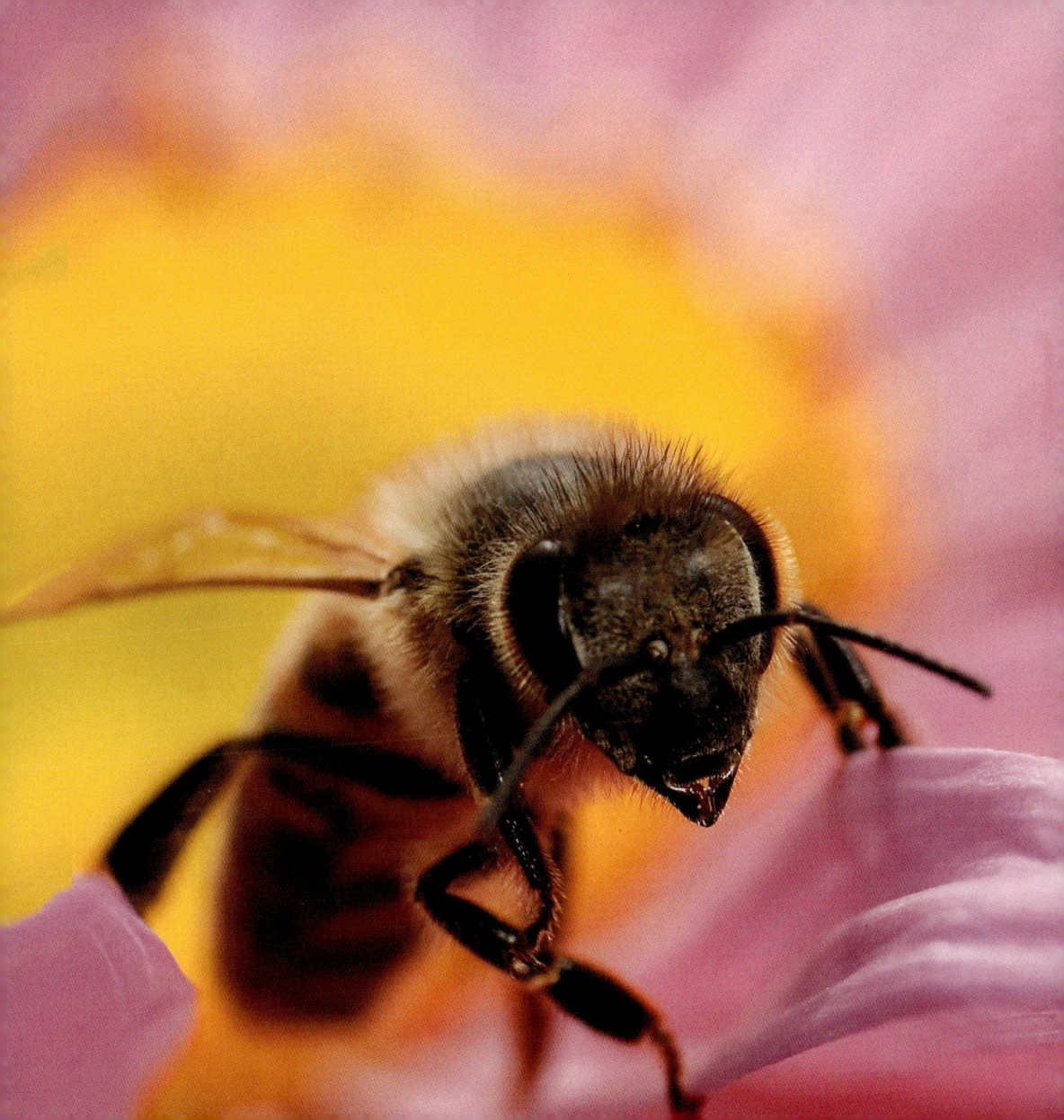

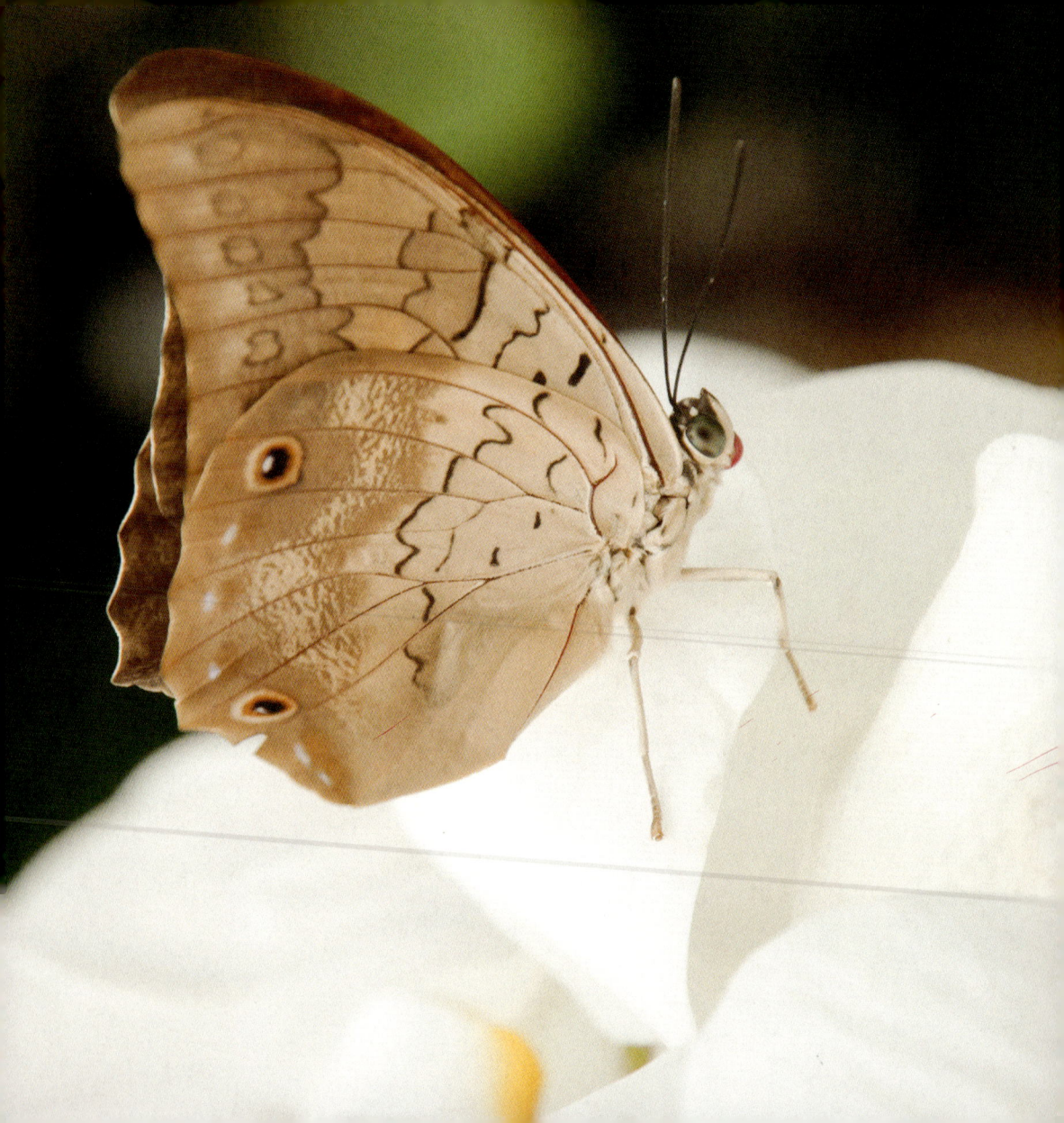

The
butterfly
counts
not
months
but
moments,
and
has
time
enough.

Rabindranath Tagore

Every kid
has a bug period.
I never
grew out of mine.

E. O. Wilson

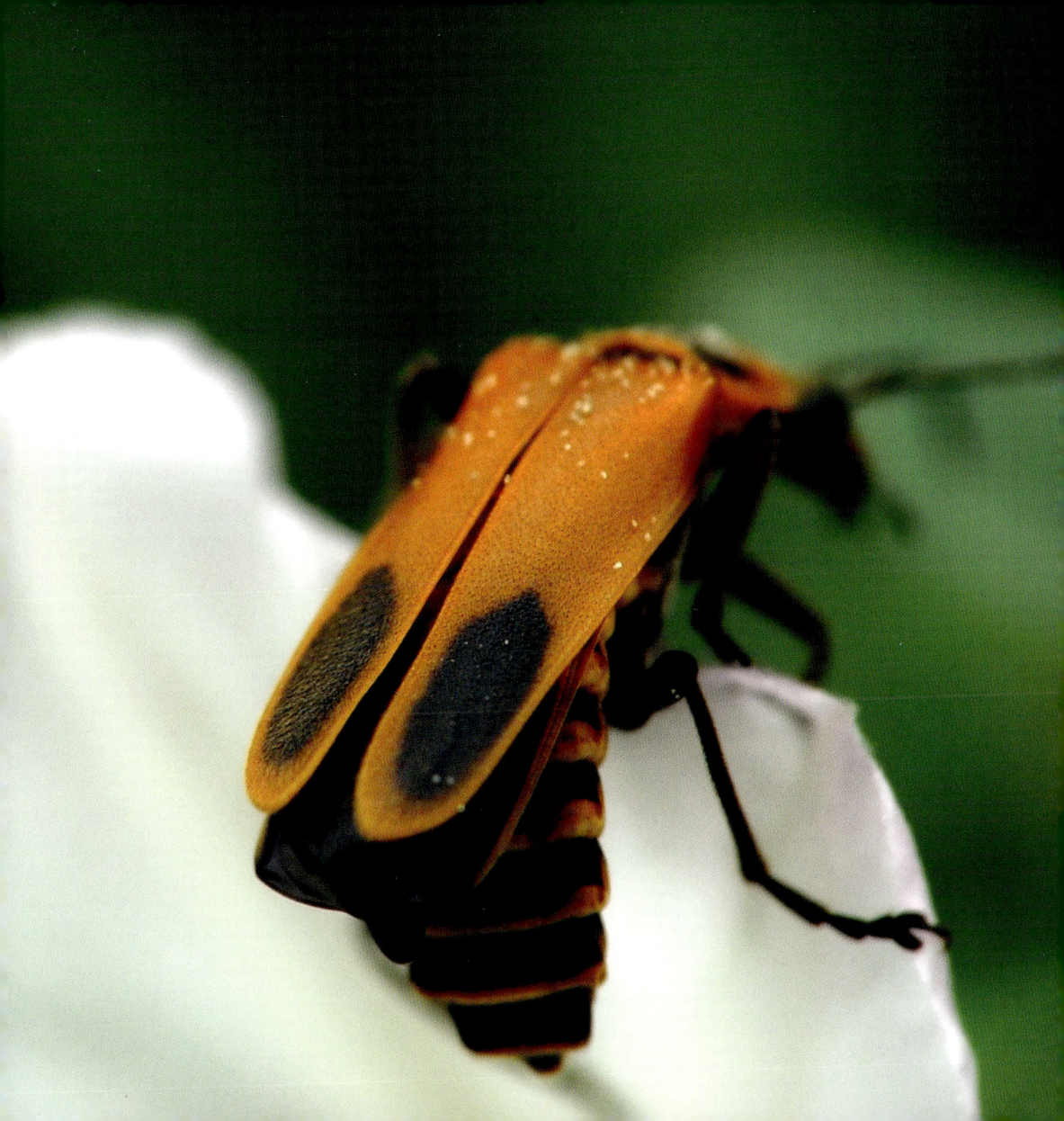

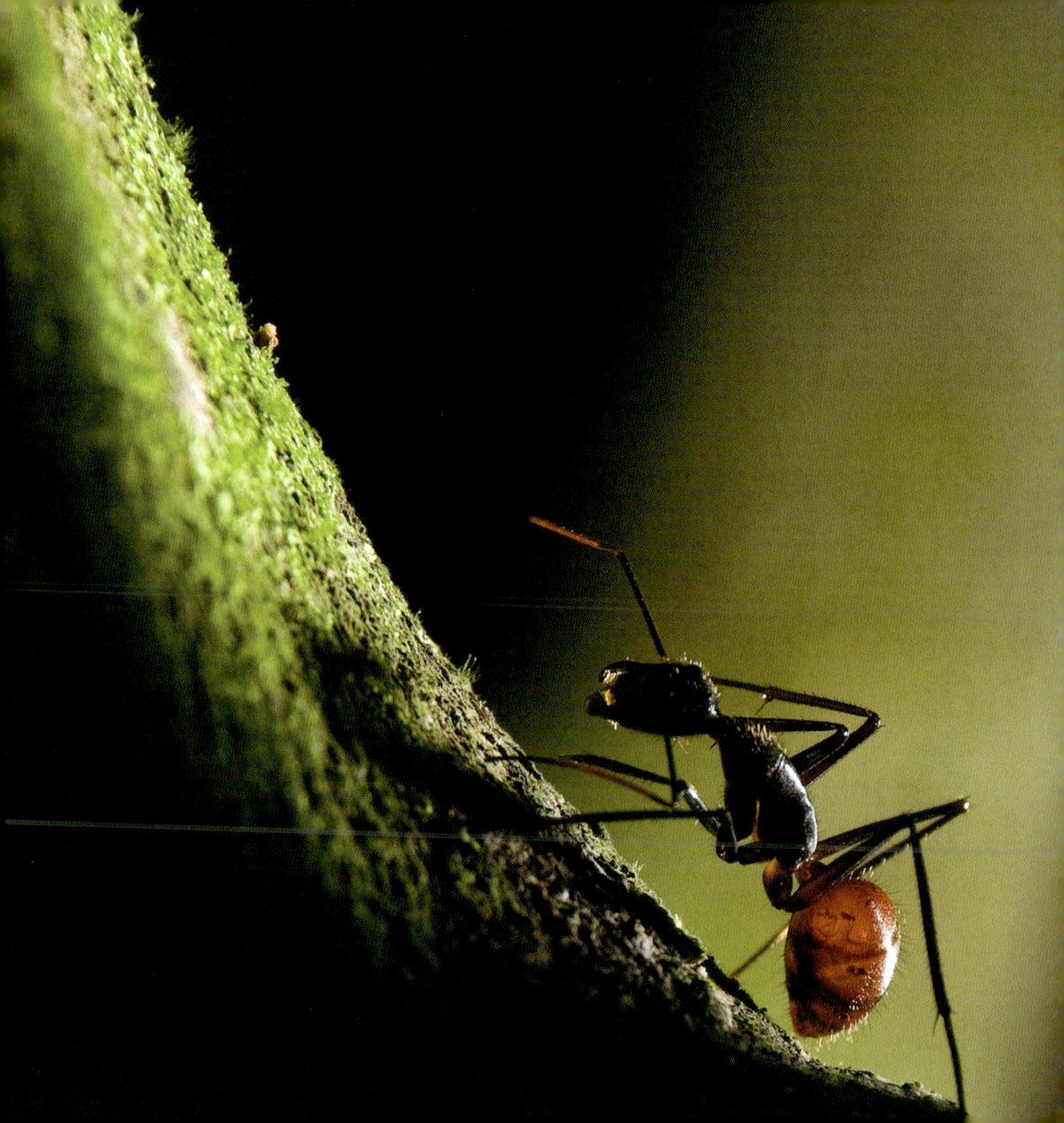

We are closer

to the ants

than to the butterflies.

Very few people

can endure

much leisure.

Gerald Brenan

All the efforts

of the

human mind

cannot

exhaust the

essence

of a single fly.

Thomas Aquinas

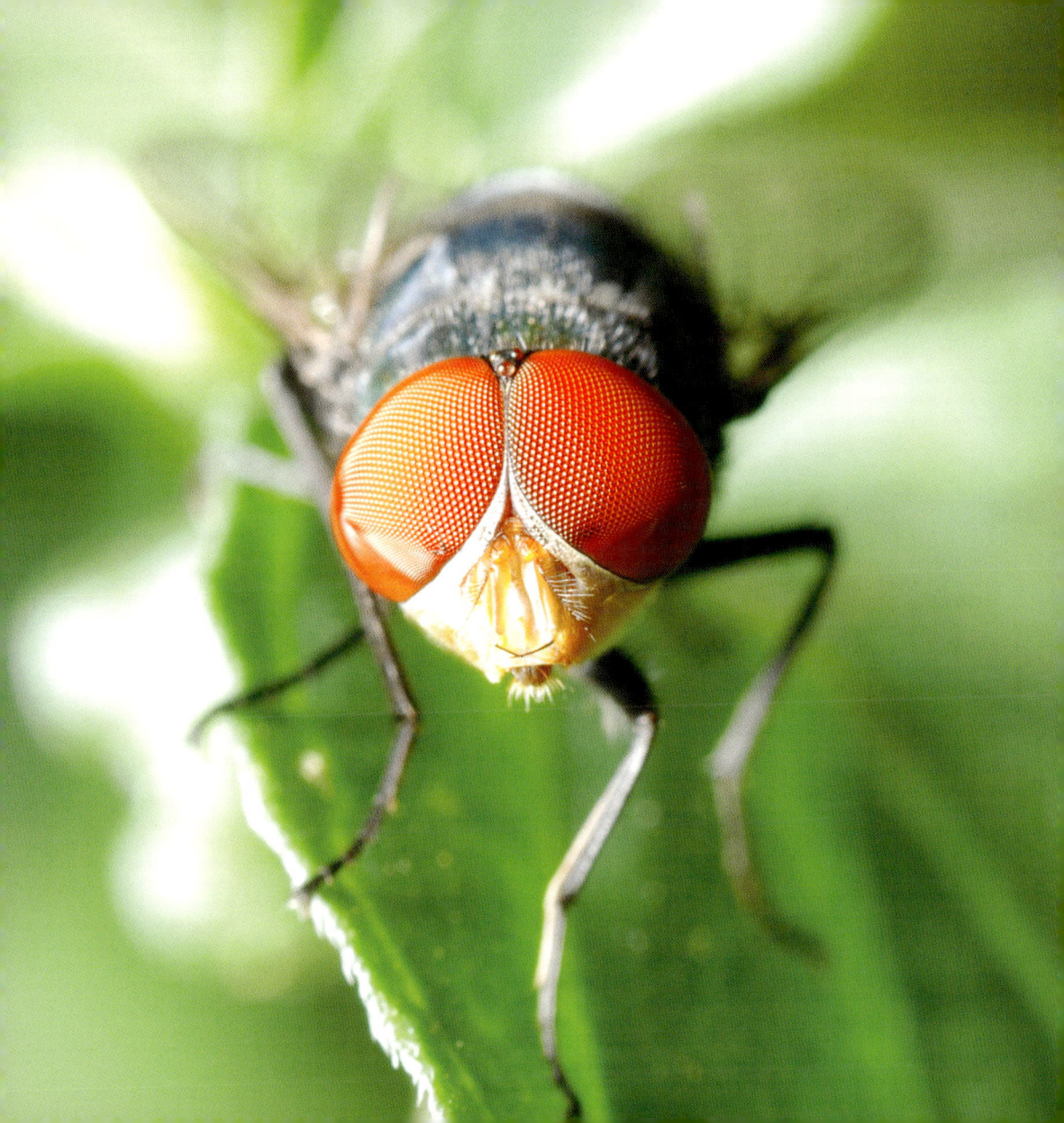

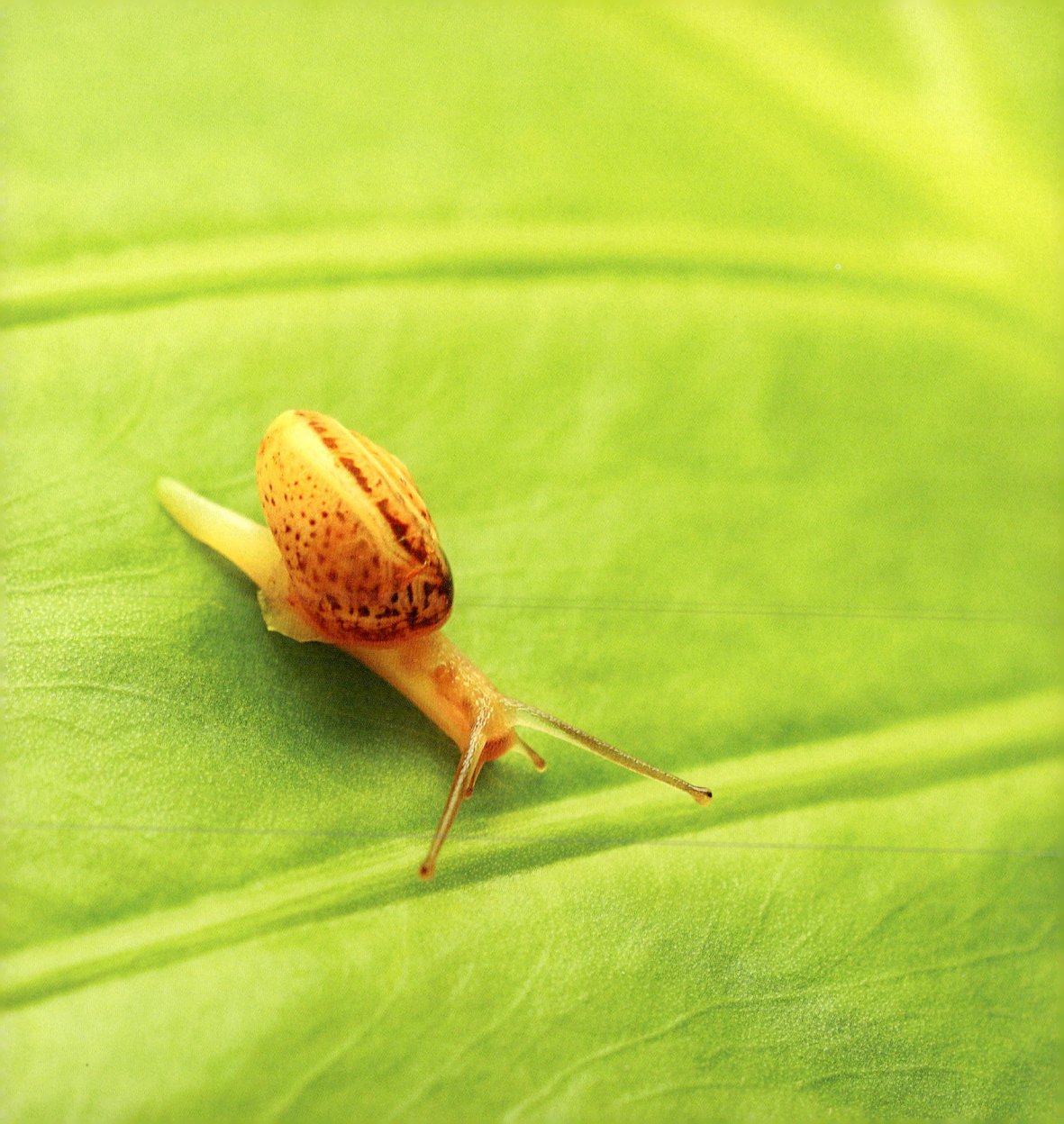

Adopt

the

pace

of

nature:

Her

secret

is

patience.

Ralph Waldo Emerson

Every blade of grass

has its ANGEL

that bends over it

and whispers,

'GROW, GROW.'

The Talmud

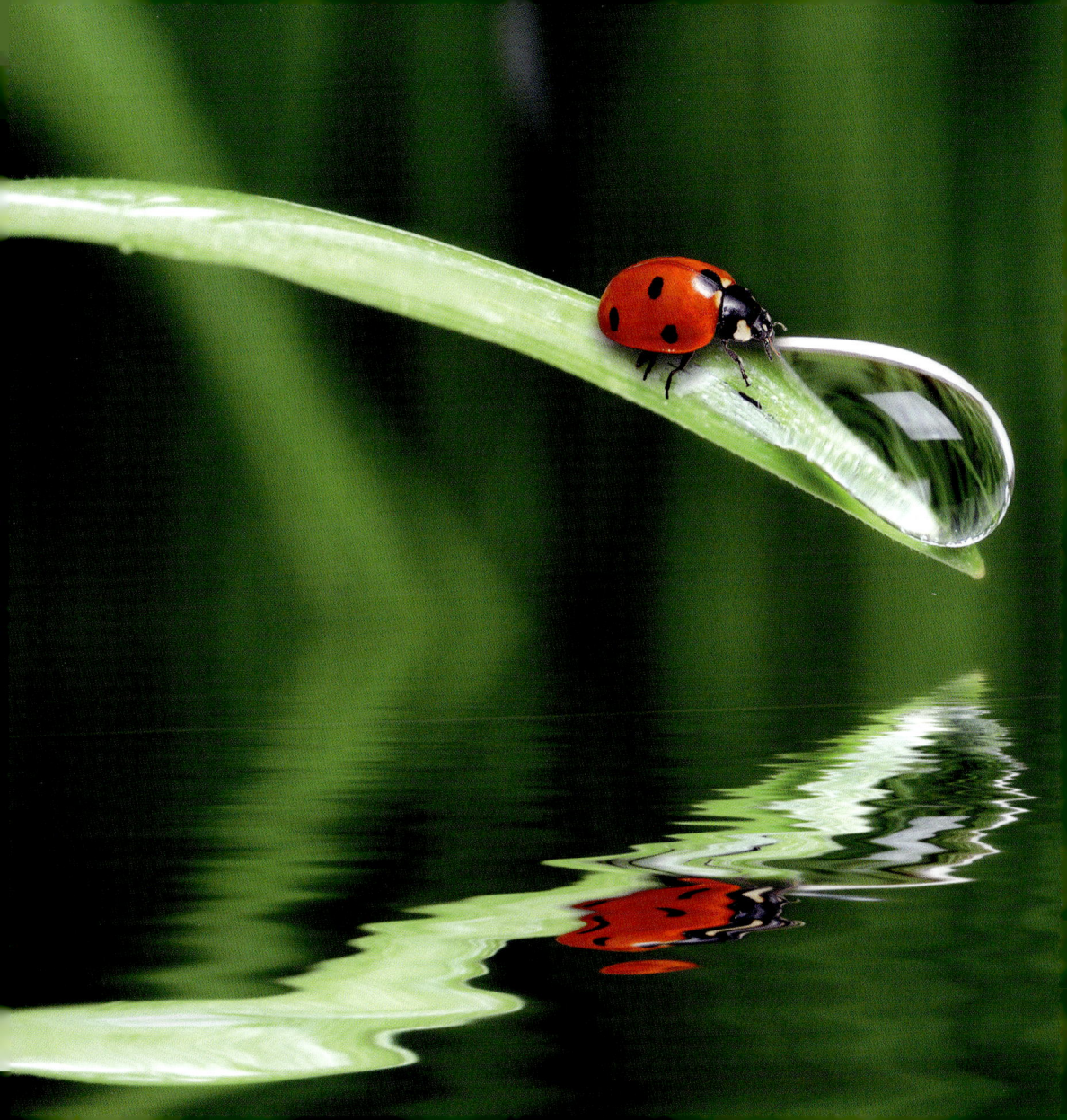

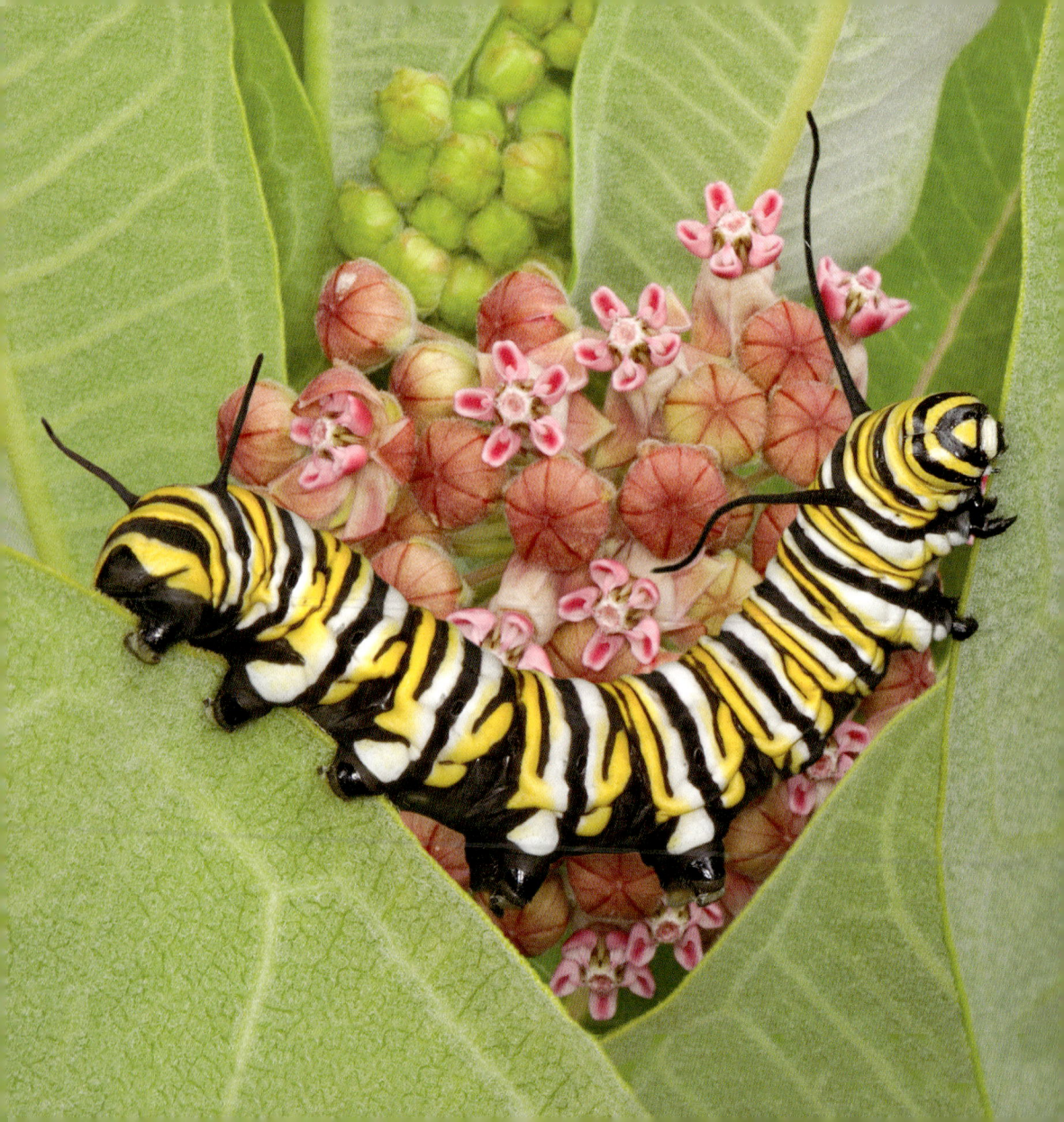

The caterpillar does all
the work but the butterfly gets all the publicity.

George Carlin

If nothing
ever
changed,
there'd be no
butterflies.

Author Unknown

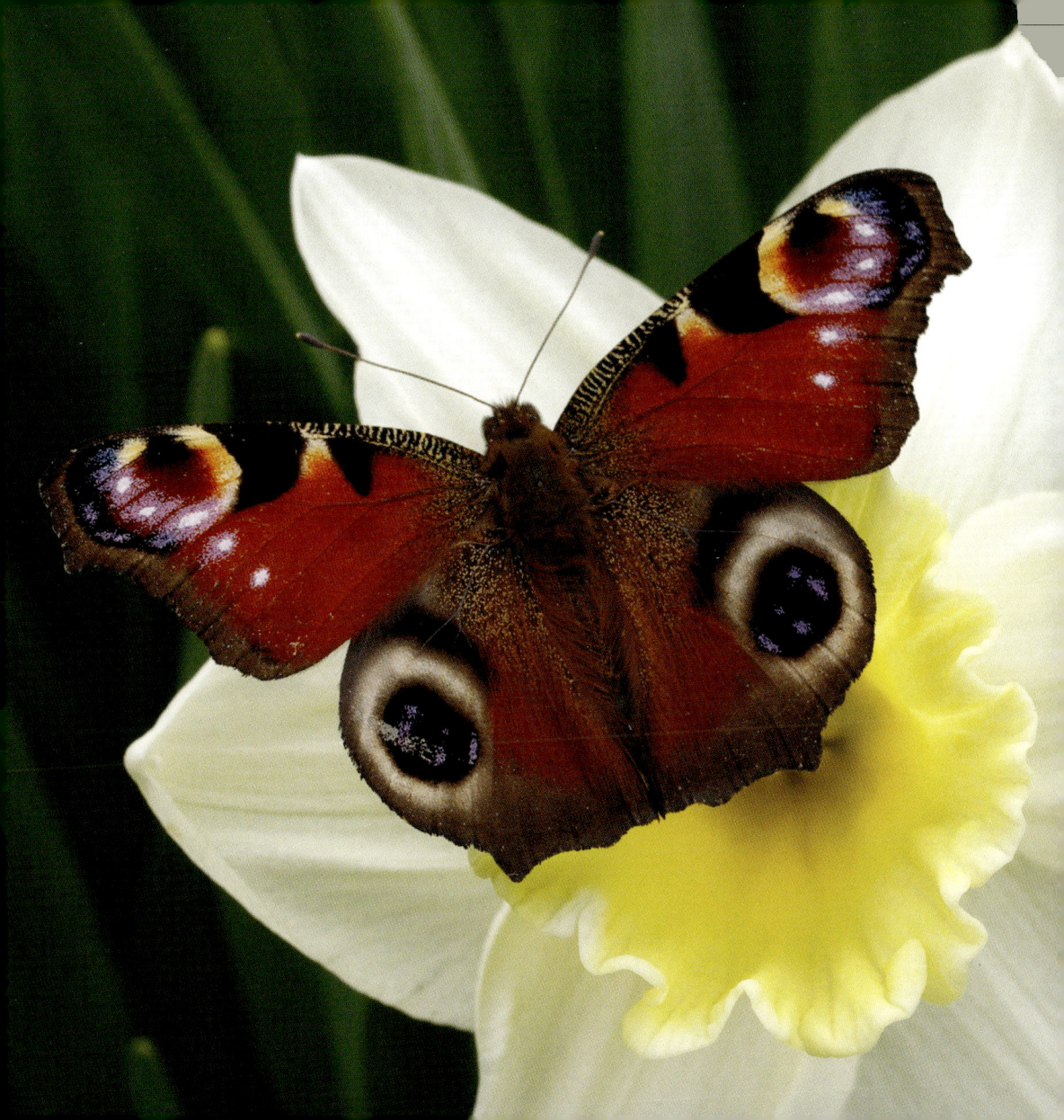

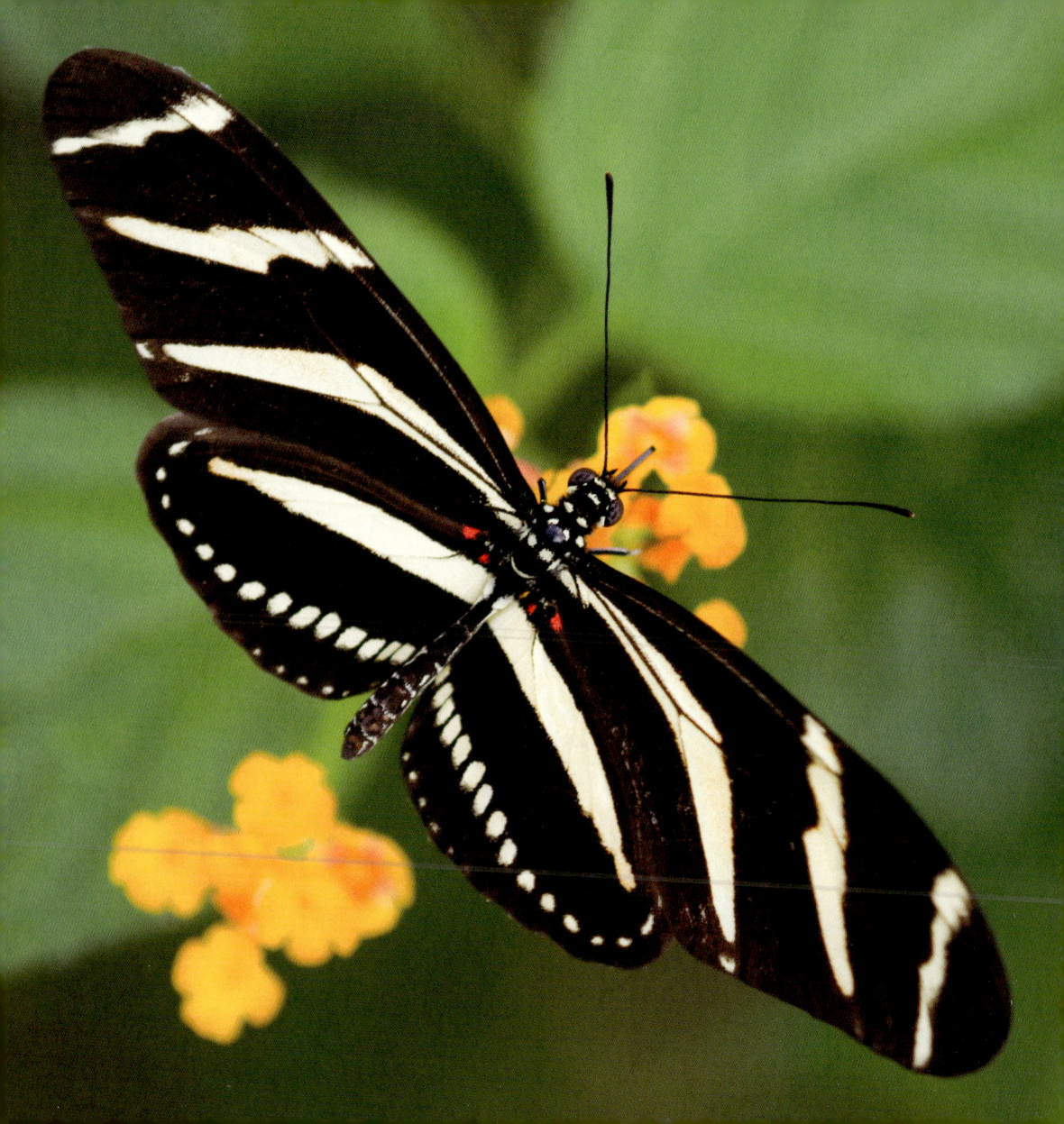

Butterflies are self propelled flowers.

R.H. Heinlein

Weeds

are

flowers too,

once

you get

to know them.

A. A. Milne

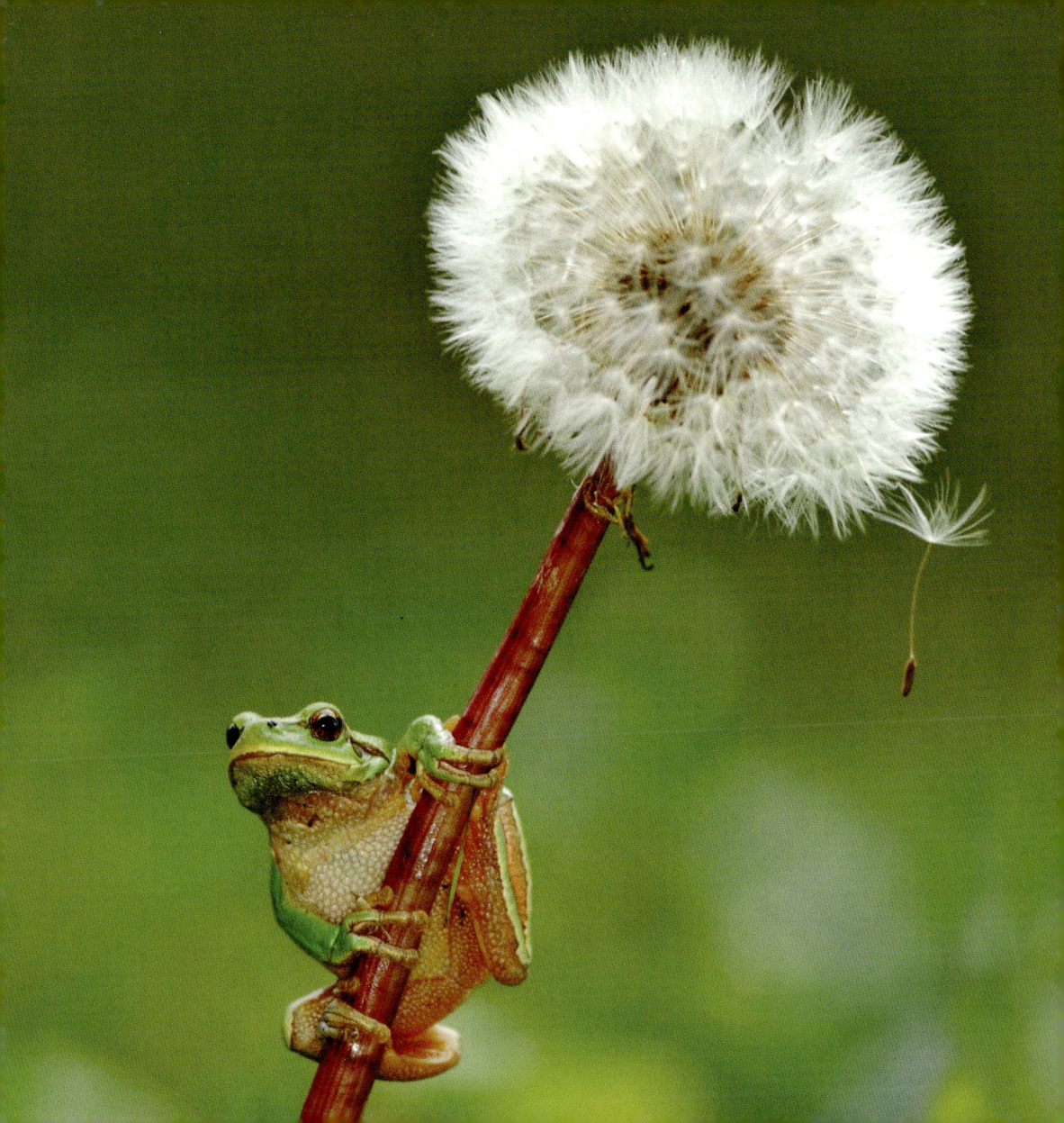

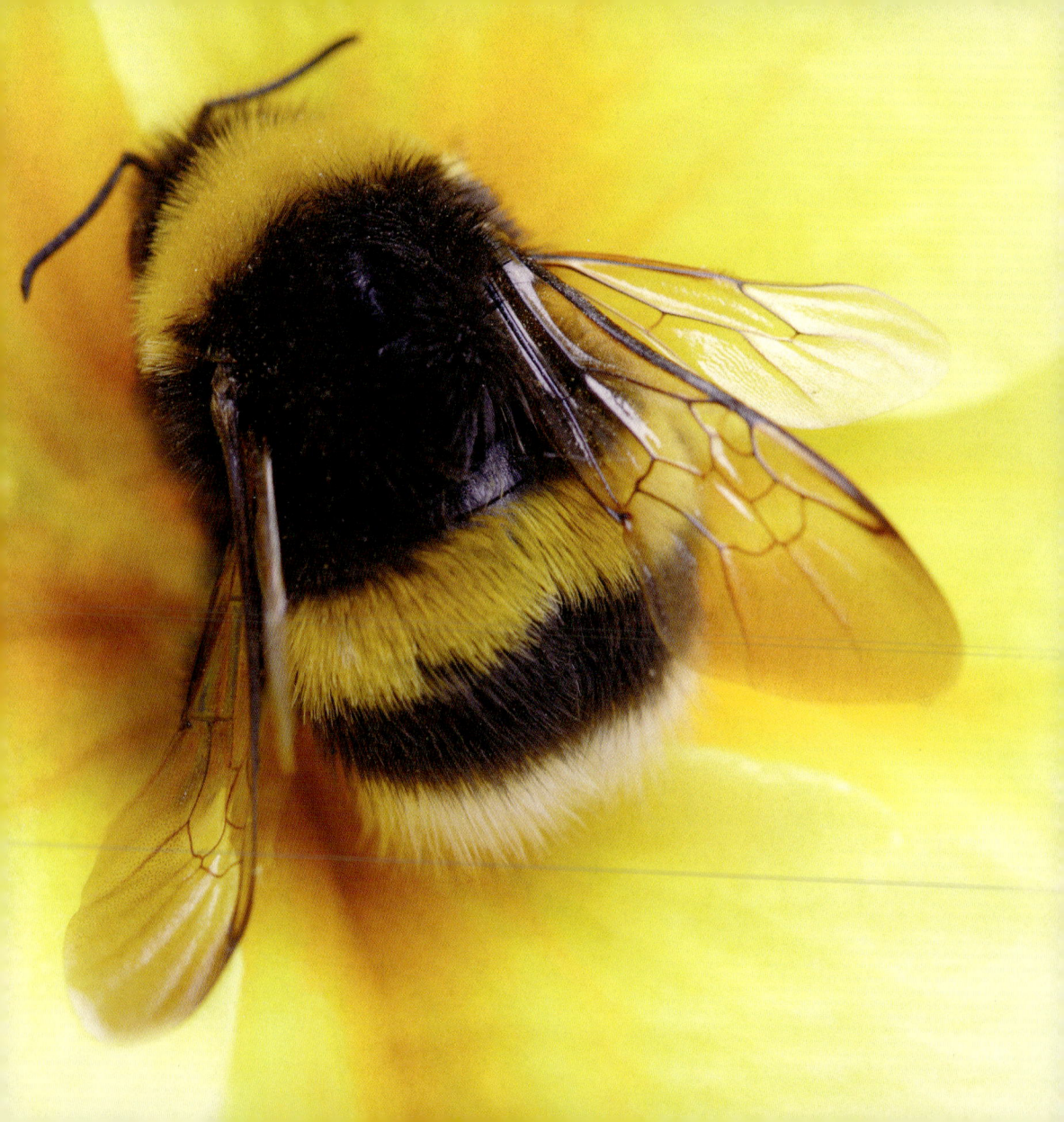

Aerodynamically,
the bumble bee shouldn't
be able to fly,
but the bumble bee
doesn't know it
so it goes on flying anyway.

Mary Kay Ash

If you think

you're too small to be effective,

you have never

been in bed with a mosquito.

Betty Reese

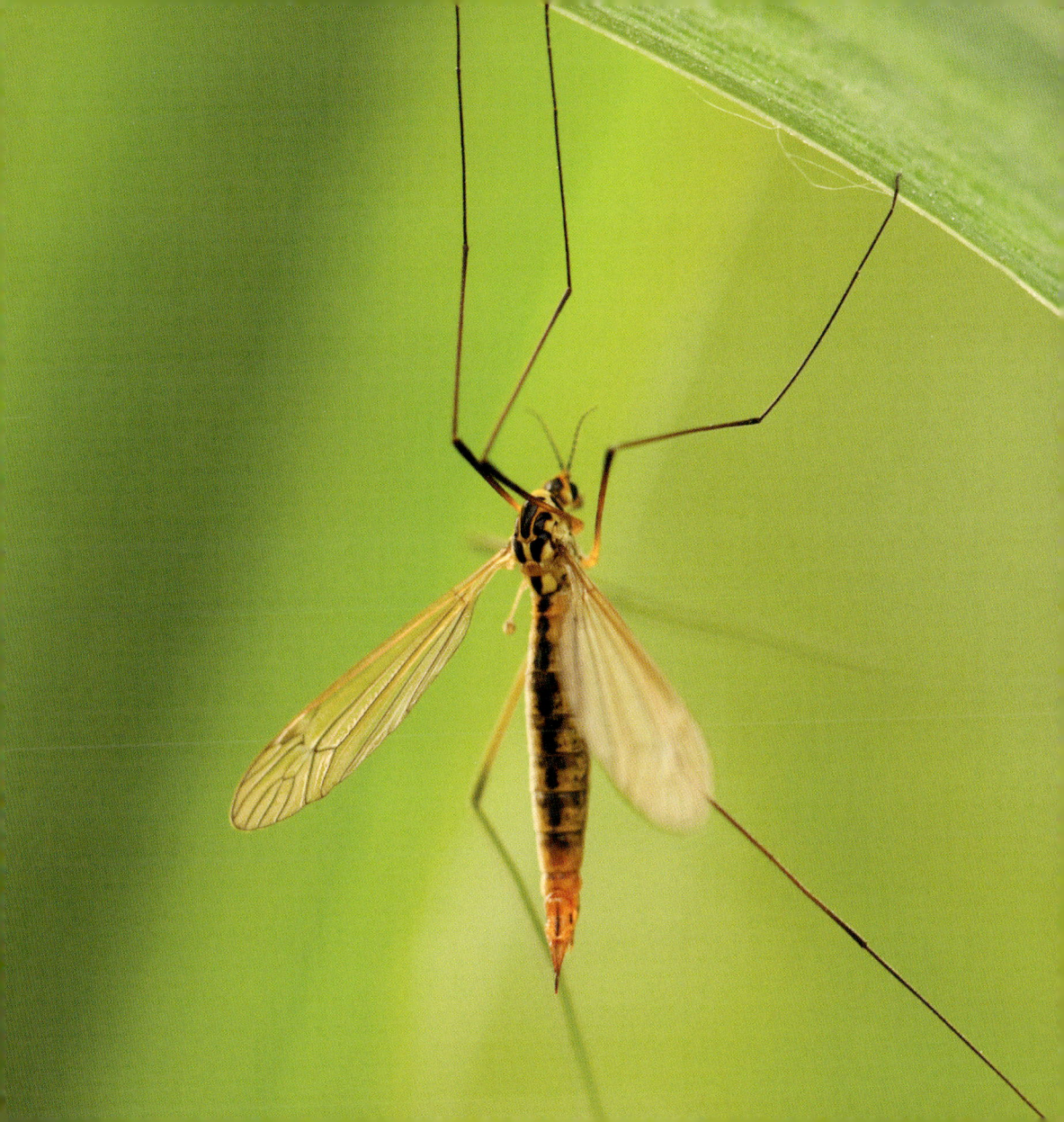

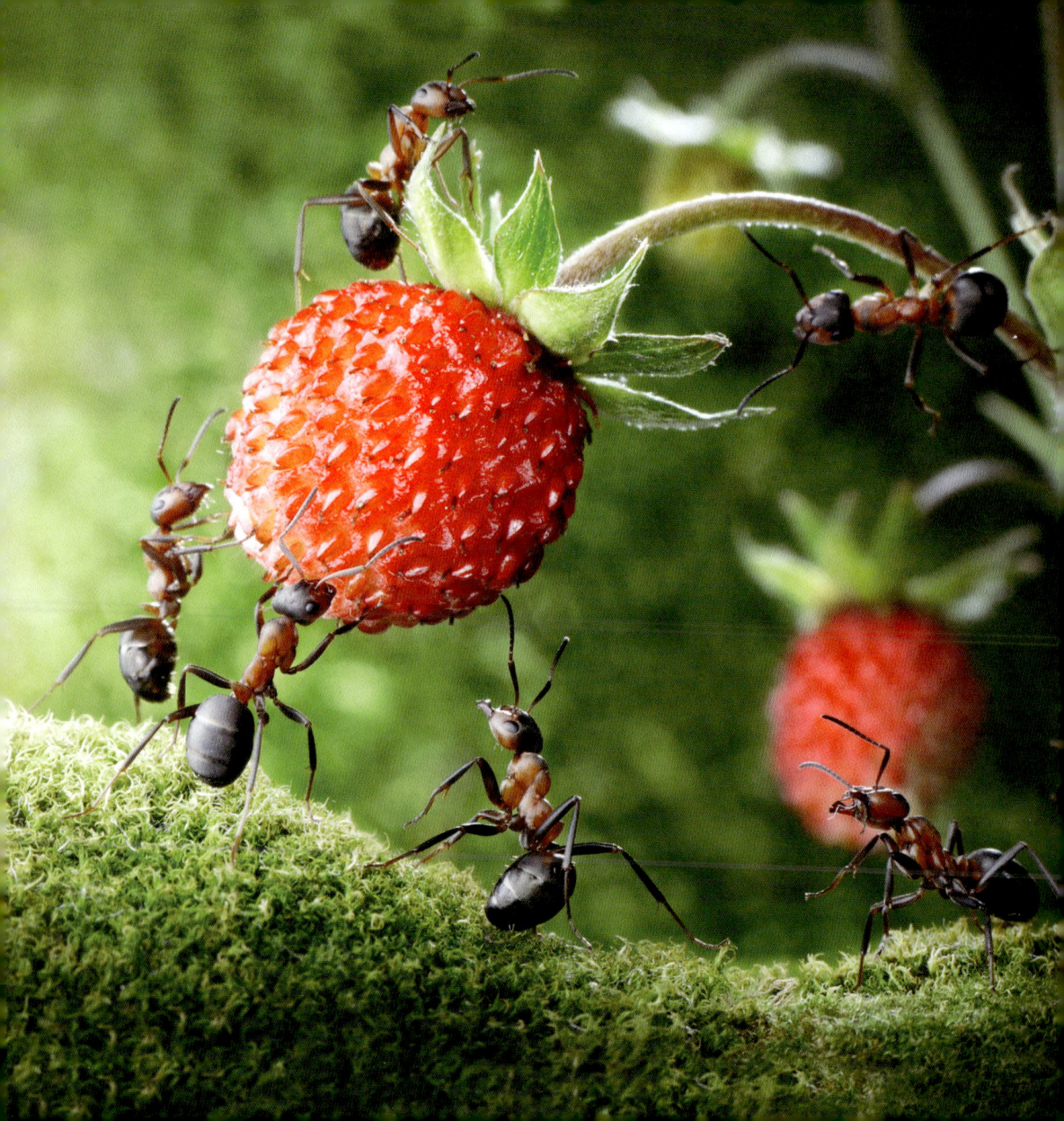

We hope that,

when the insects take over

the world,

they will remember

with gratitude

how we took them along

on all our picnics.

Bill Vaughan

The mosquito

is the state bird of New Jersey.

Andy Warhol

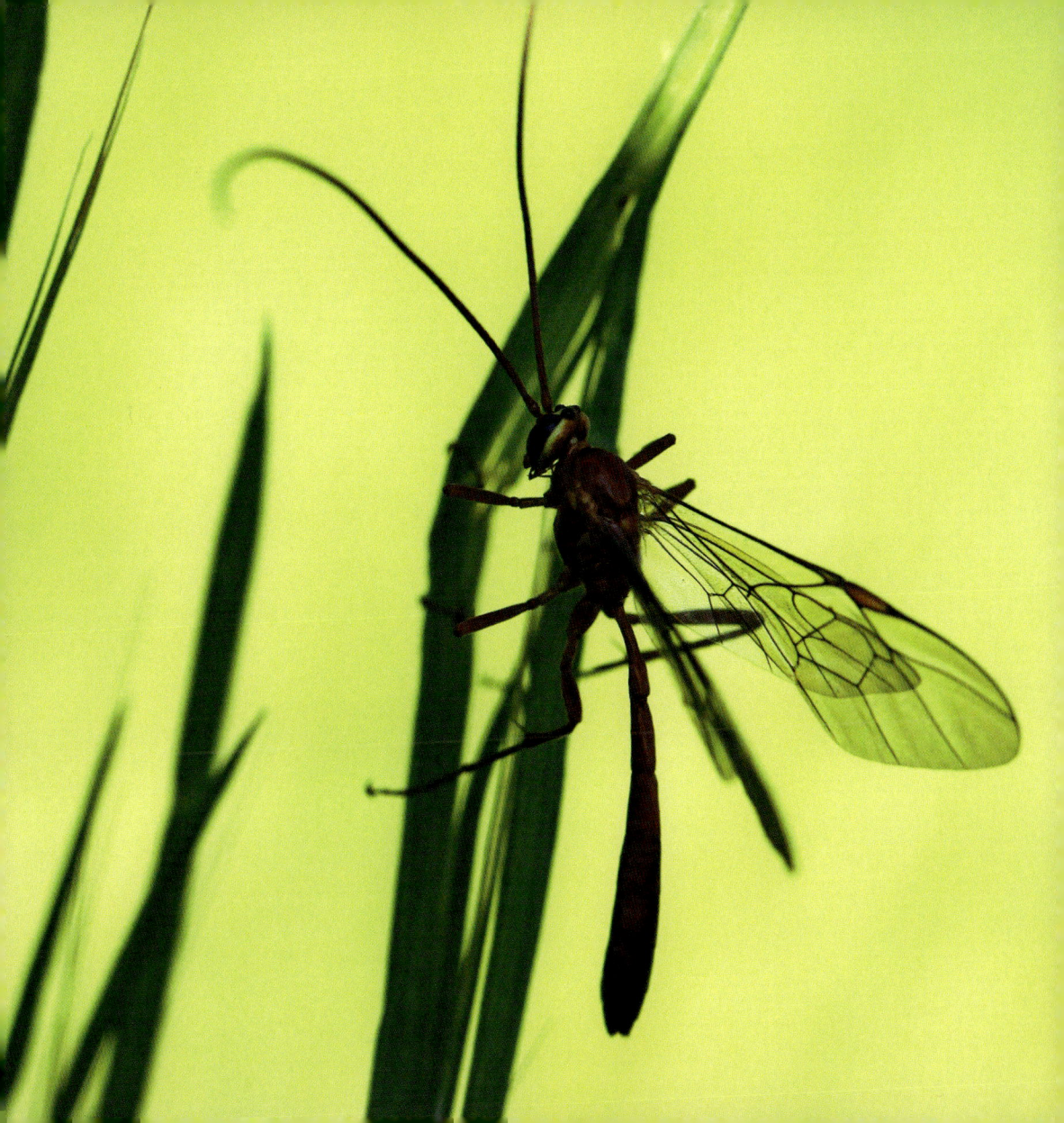

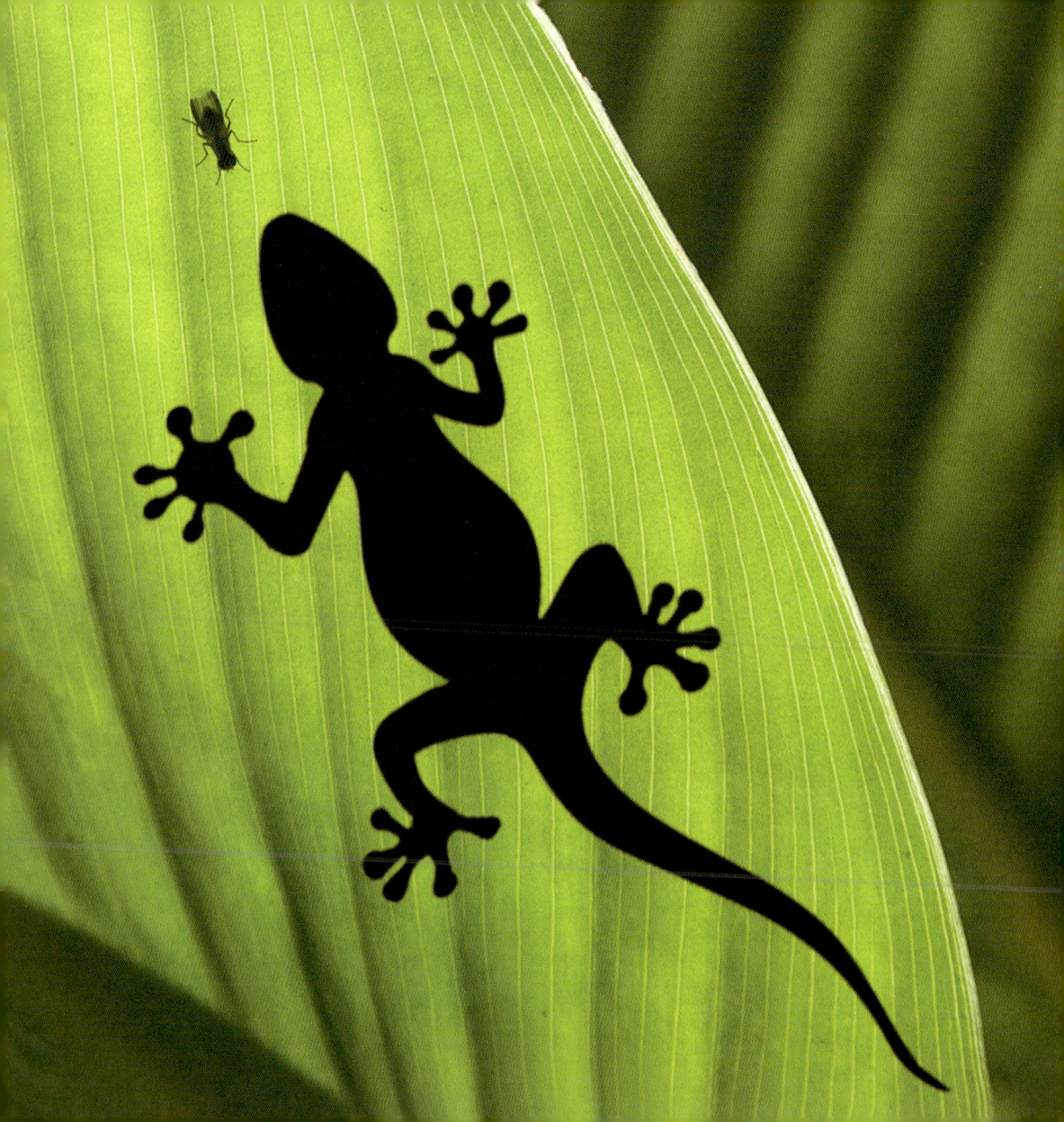

Why didn't Noah swat those two mosquitoes?

Author Unknown

The perception of beauty is a moral test.

Henry David Thoreau

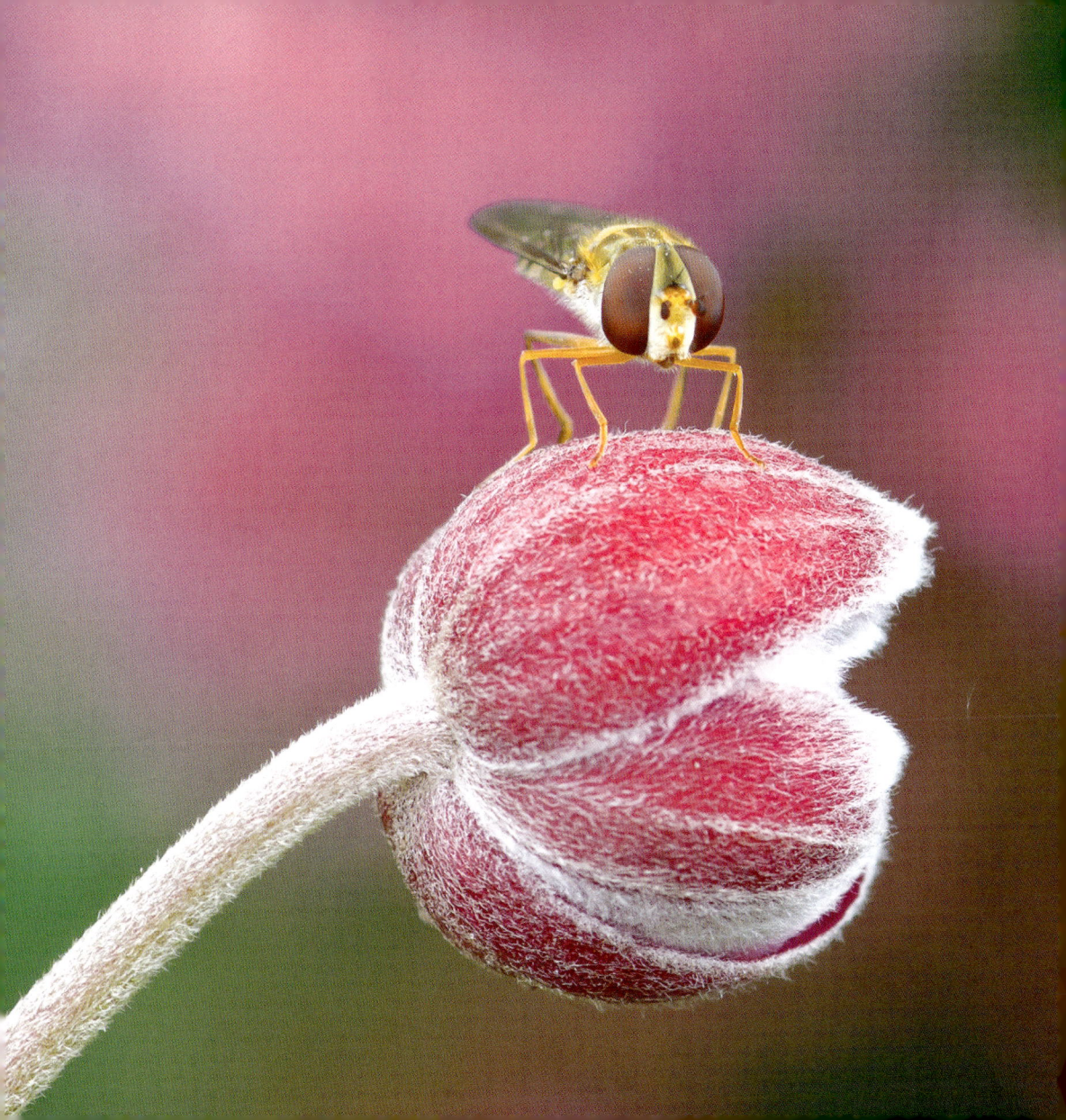

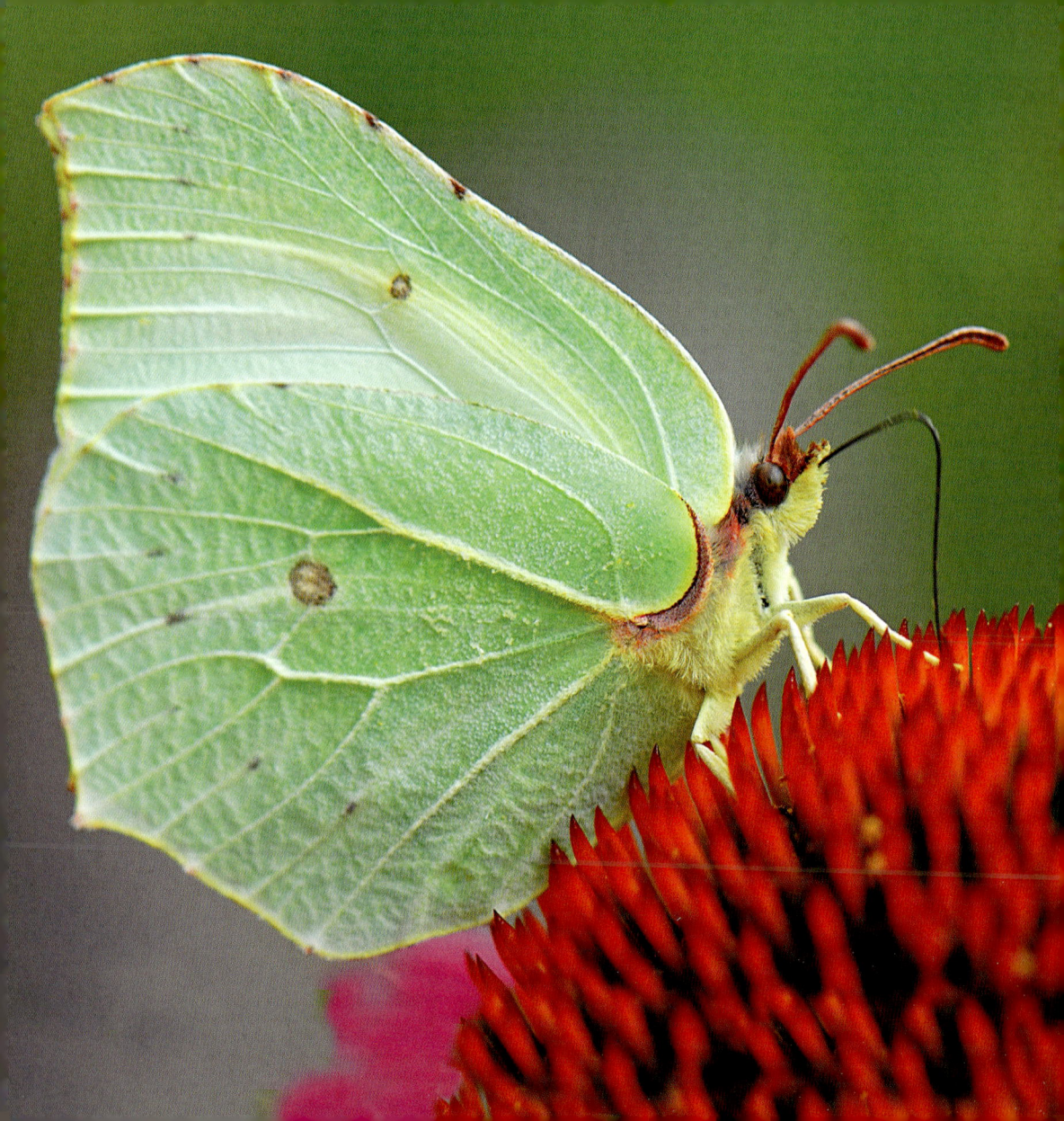

Everything has beauty, but
not everyone sees it.

Confucius

Life is infinitely stranger

than anything

which the mind of man

could invent.

We would not dare

to conceive the things

which are really

mere commonplaces

of existence.

Arthur Conan Doyle

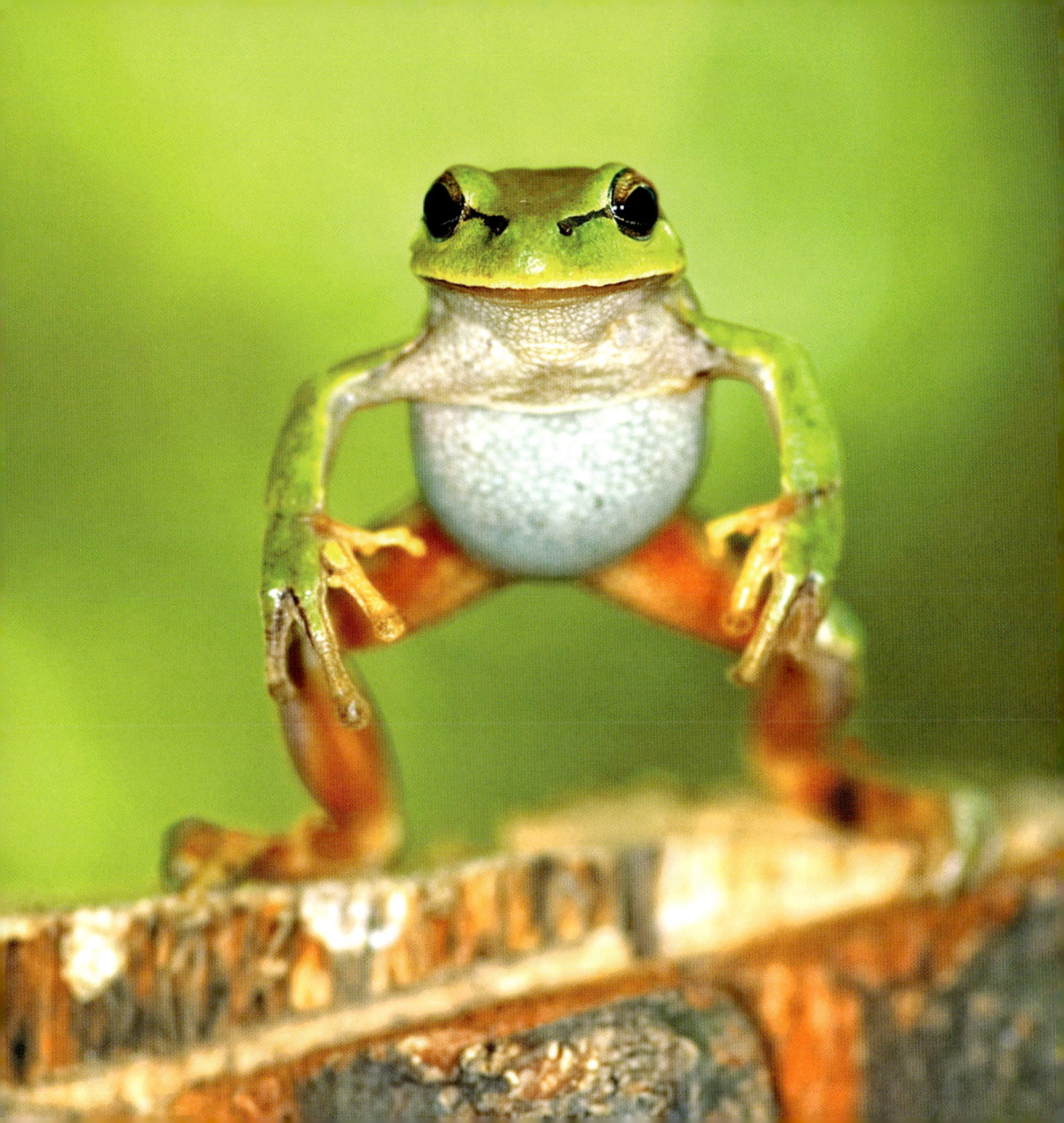

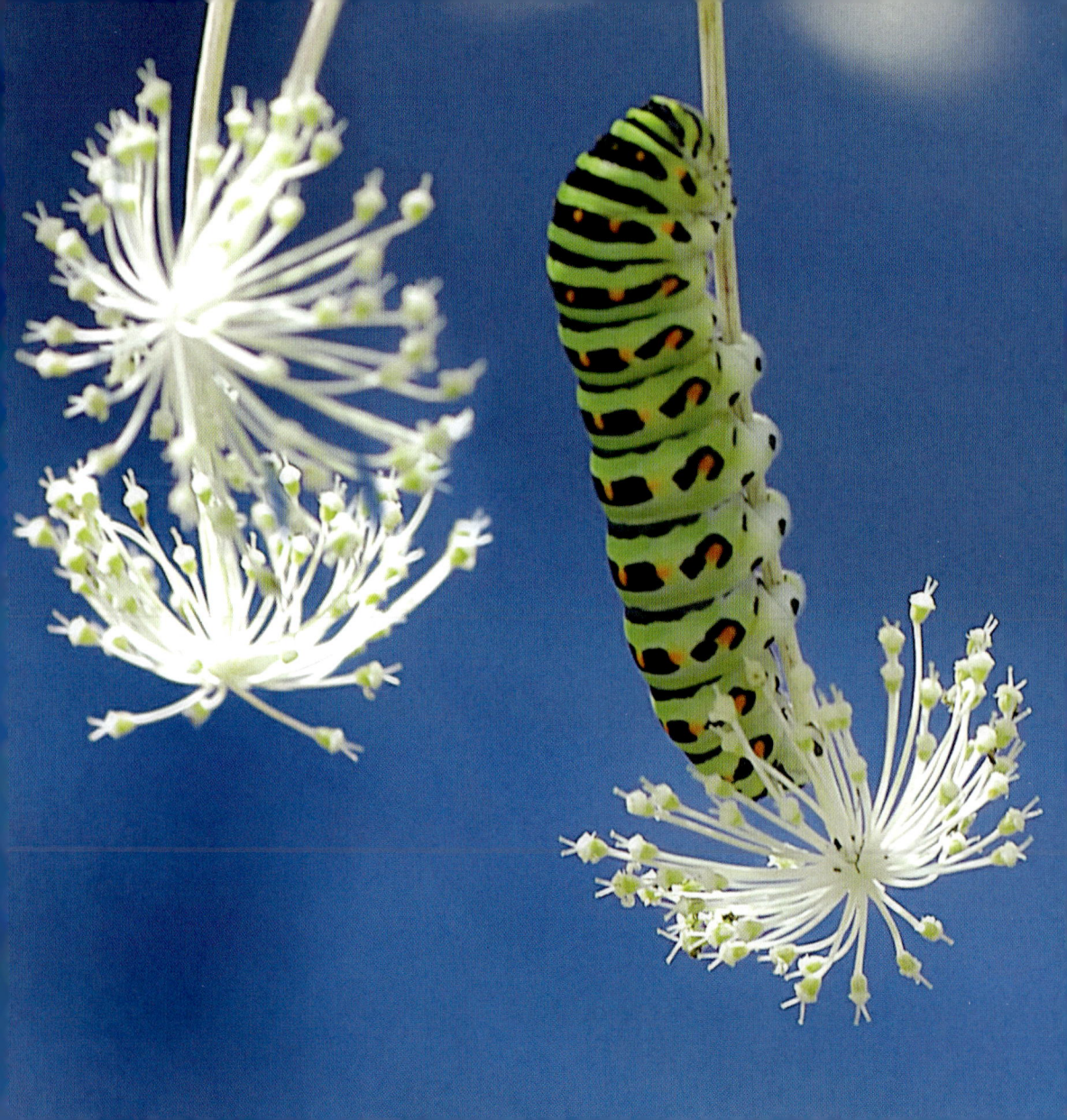

There is

nothing in a caterpillar

that tells you

it's going to be a butterfly.

R. Buckminster Fuller

And this, our life,

exempt from public haunt,

finds tongues in trees,

books in the running brooks,

sermons in stones,

and good in everything.

William Shakespeare

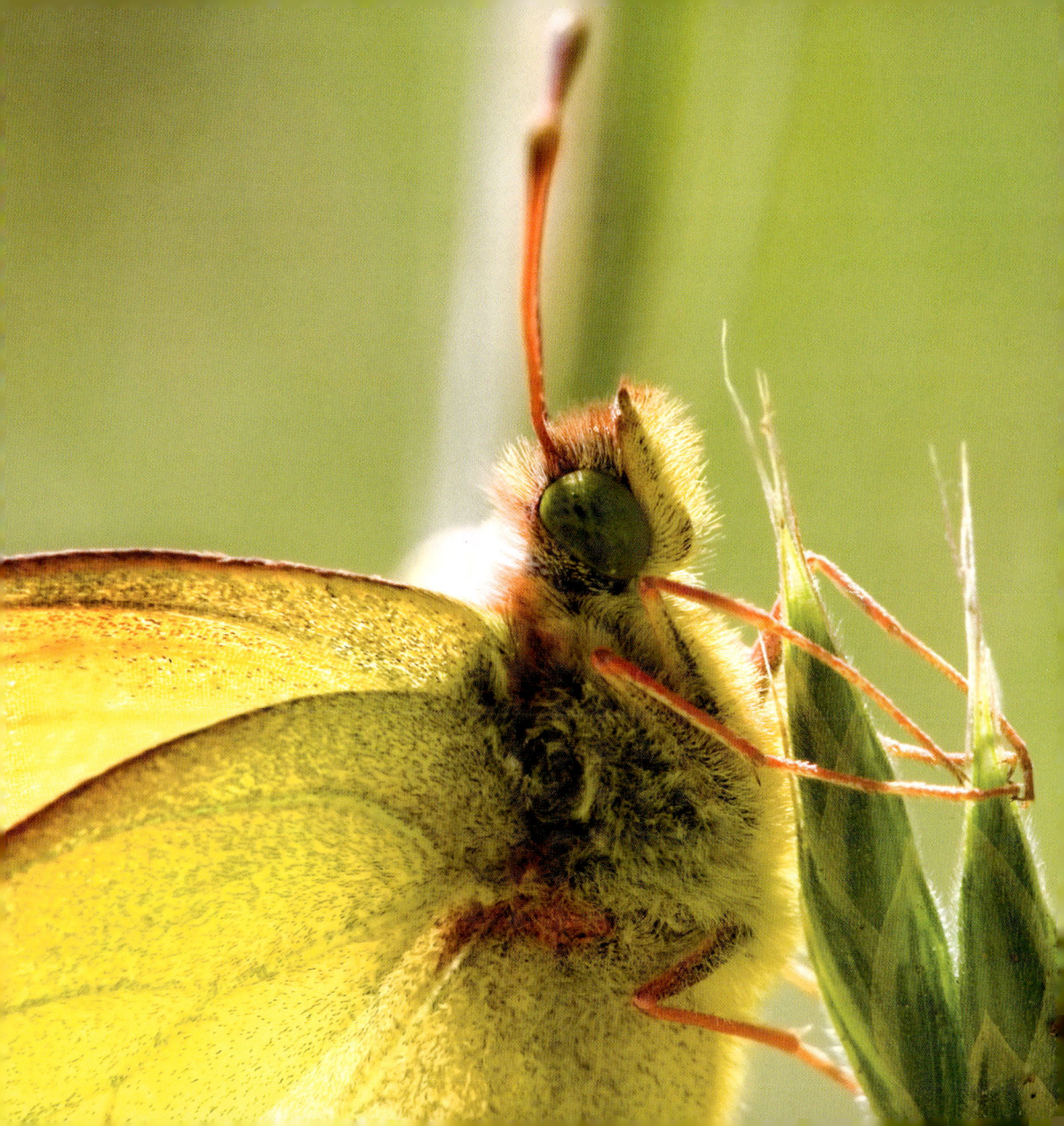

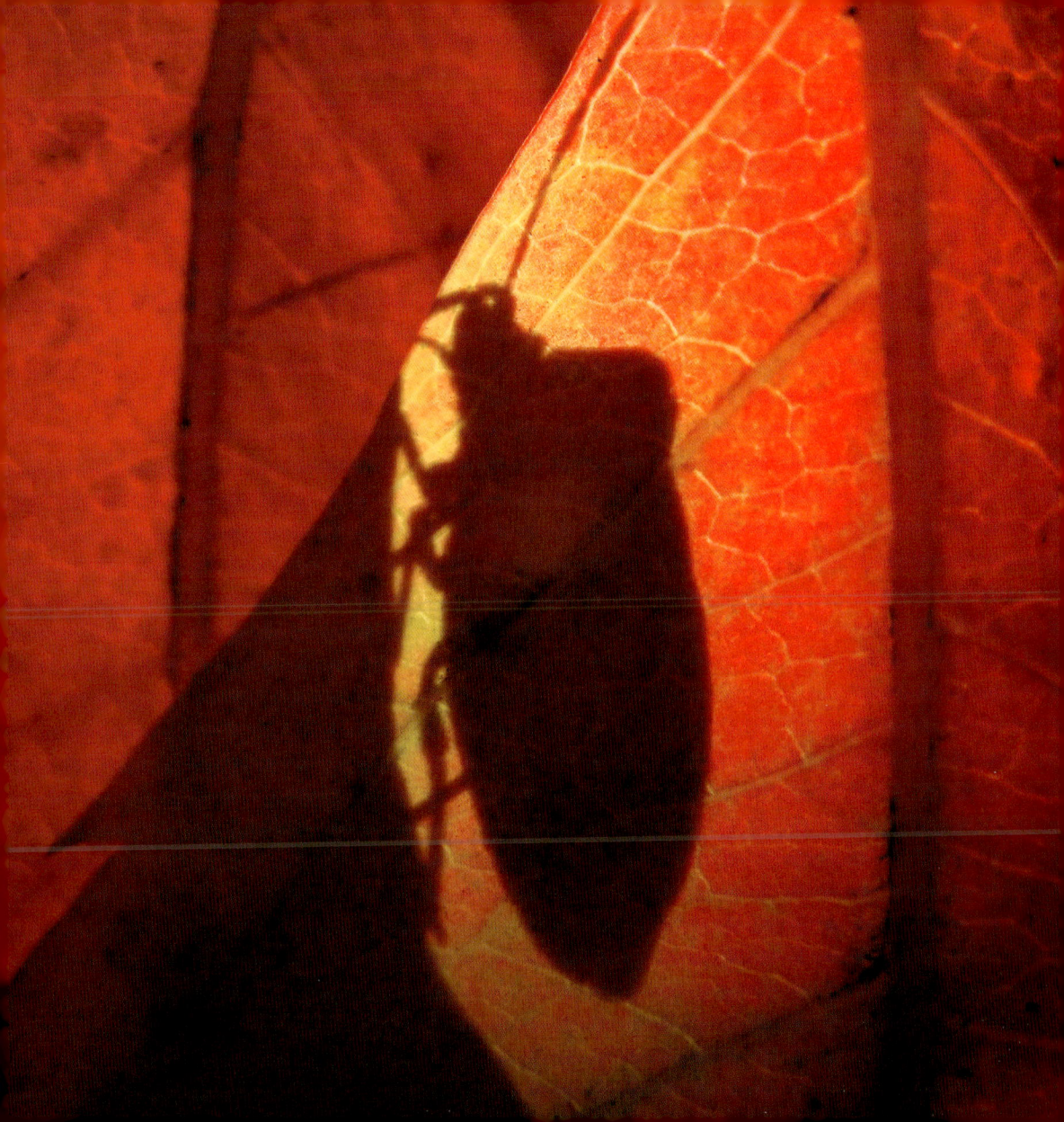

Autumn

is a second spring

when every leaf

is a flower.

Albert Camus

Crimson

      pepper pod

add two

    pairs of wings

and look

       darting

dragonfly.

Matsuo Basho

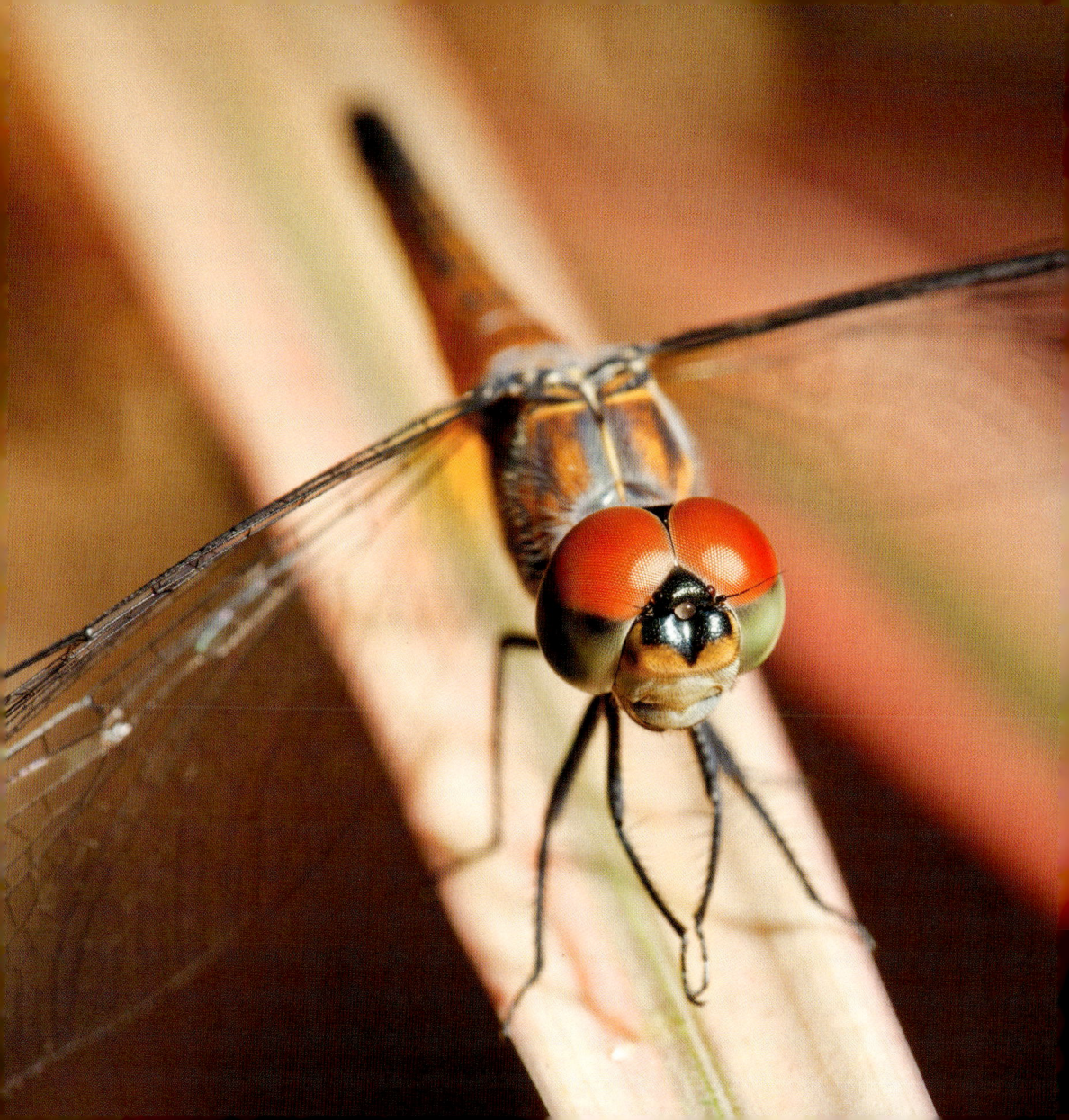

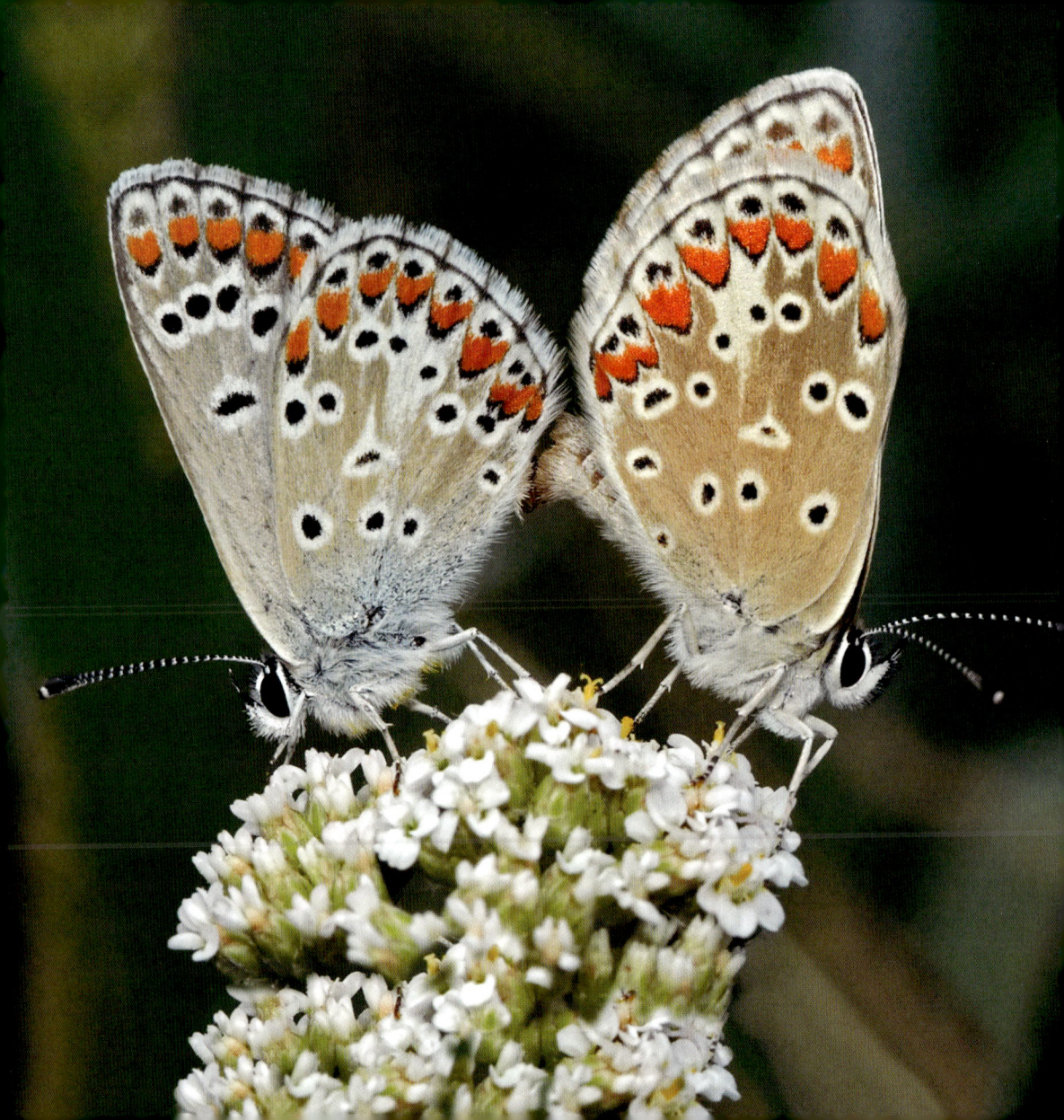

I dreamed
I was a butterfly,
flitting around in the sky;
then I awoke.
Now I wonder:

    Am I a man

        who dreamt

    of being

a butterfly, or

        am I a butterfly

    dreaming

        that I am

a man?

Zhuangzi

The higher we soar

the smaller we appear to those

who cannot fly.

Friedrich Nietzsche

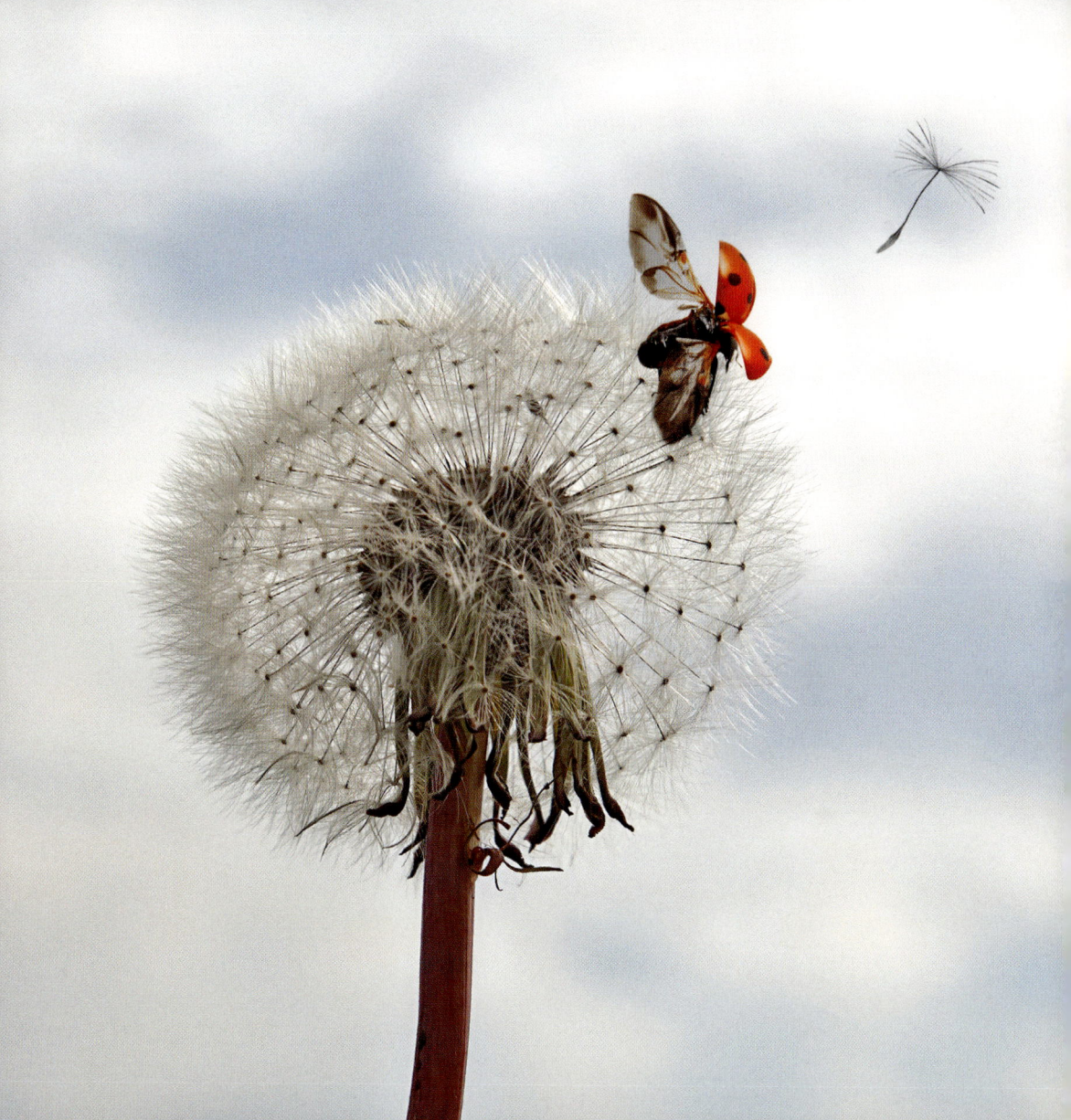

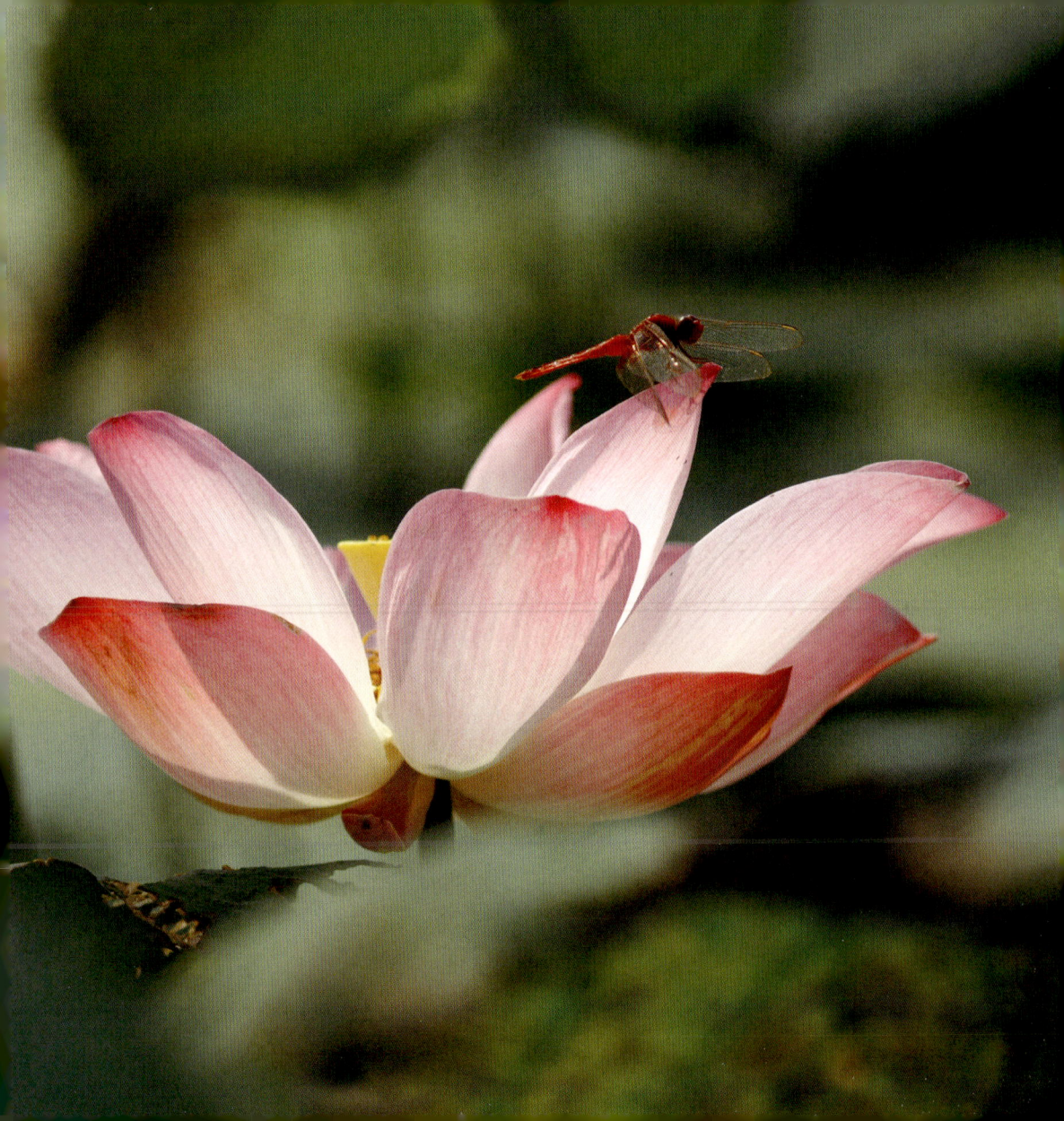

Our task must be

to free ourselves from this prison

by widening our circle

of compassion, to embrace

all living creatures and the whole

of nature in its beauty.

Albert Einstein

Beauty in things exists

in the mind

which contemplates them.

David Hume

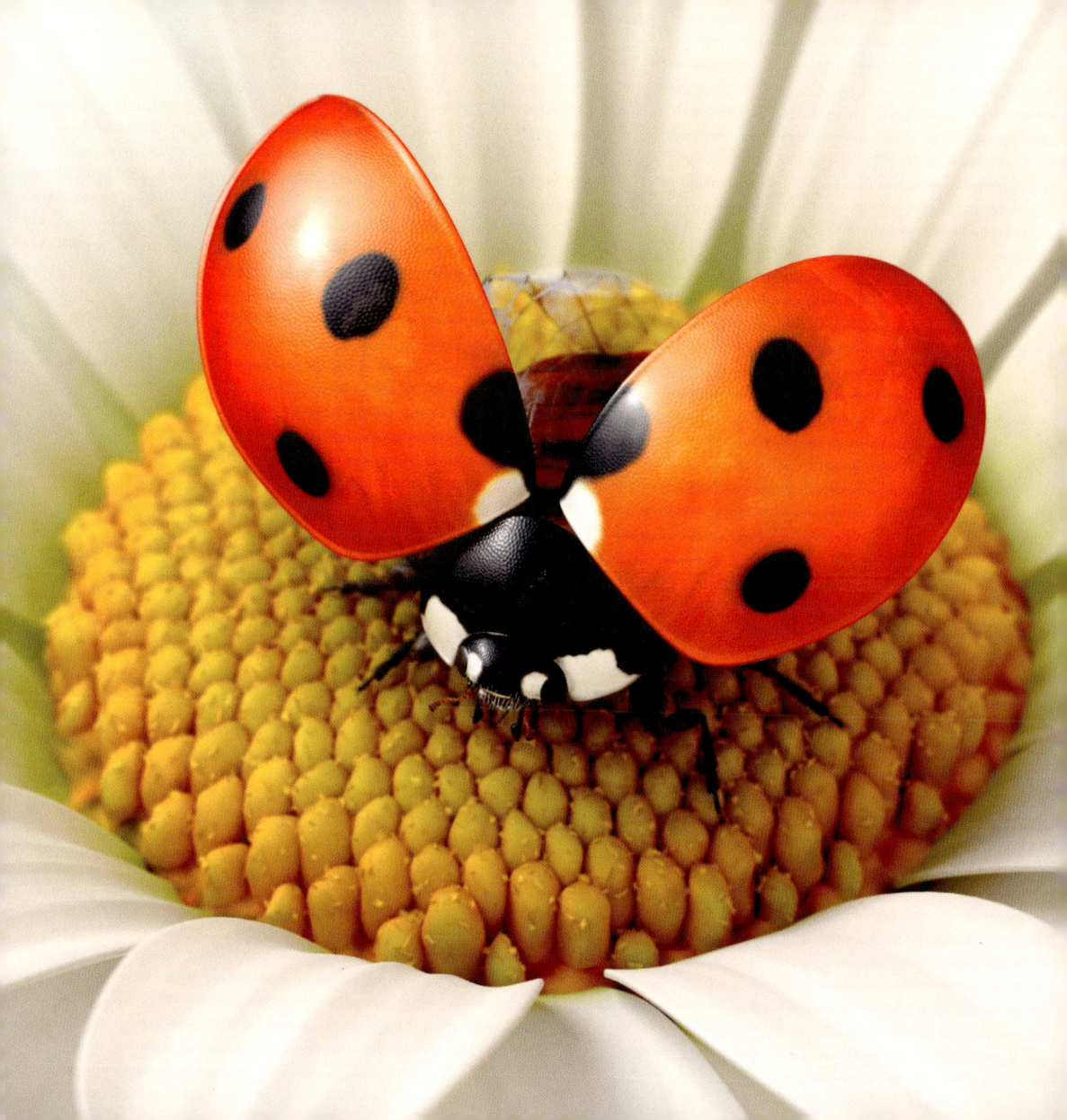

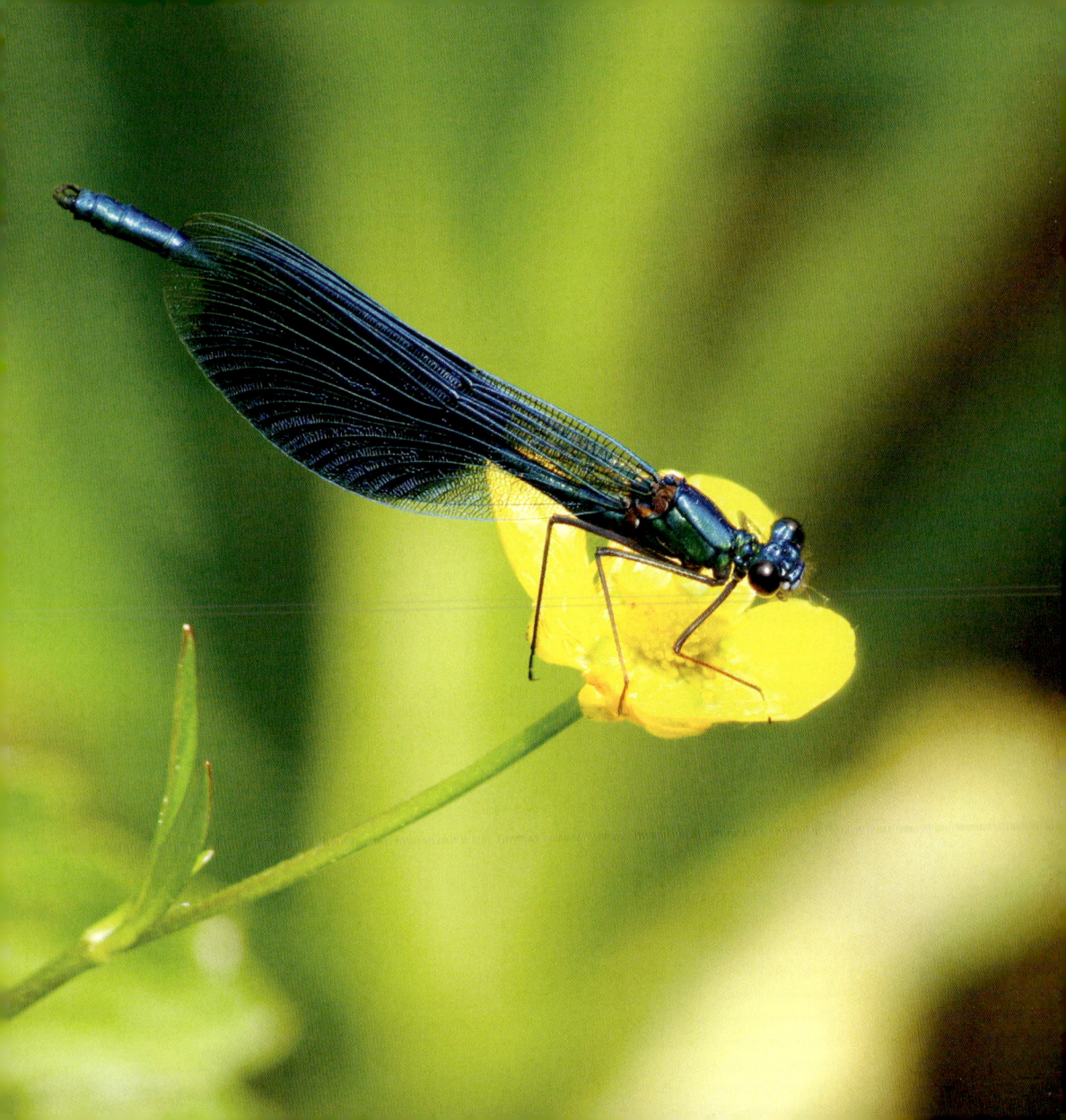

Look deep into nature,

and then you will understand everything better.

Albert Einstein

Sadness

flies

away

on

the

wings

of

time.

Jean de La Fontaine

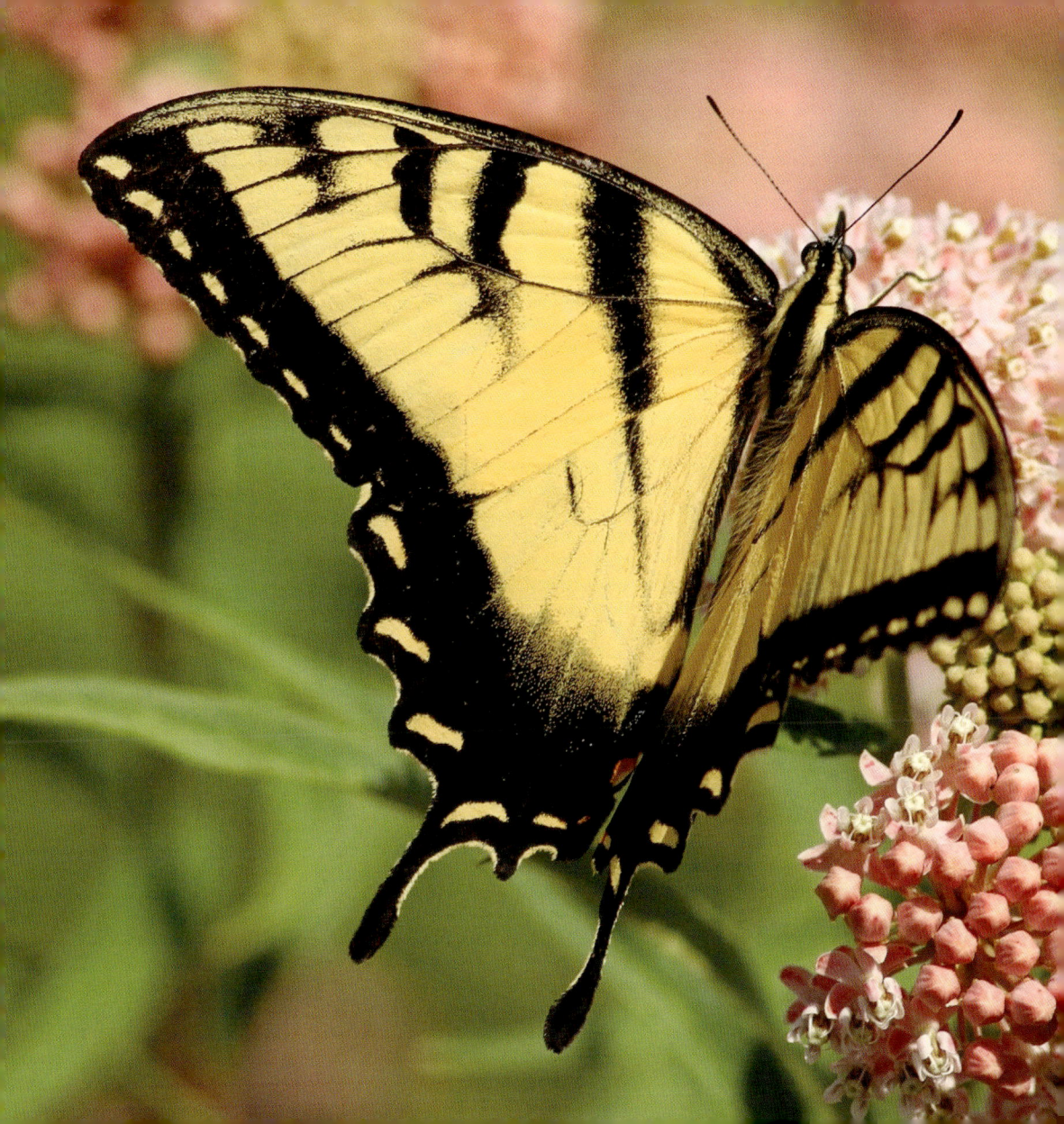

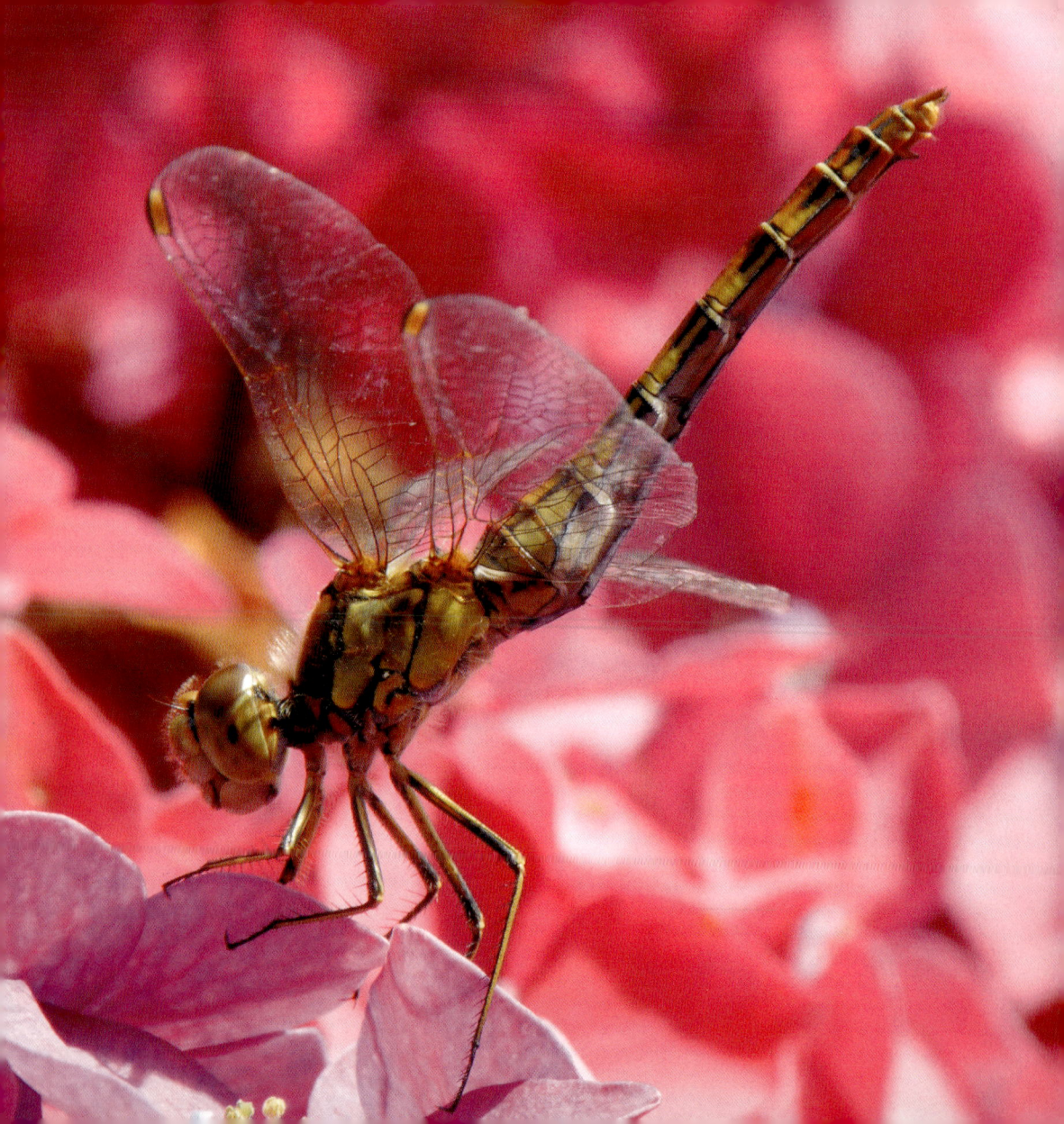

Never believe that a few
caring people
can't change the world.
For, indeed,
that's all who ever have.

Margaret Mead

Garden as though you will live forever.

William Kent

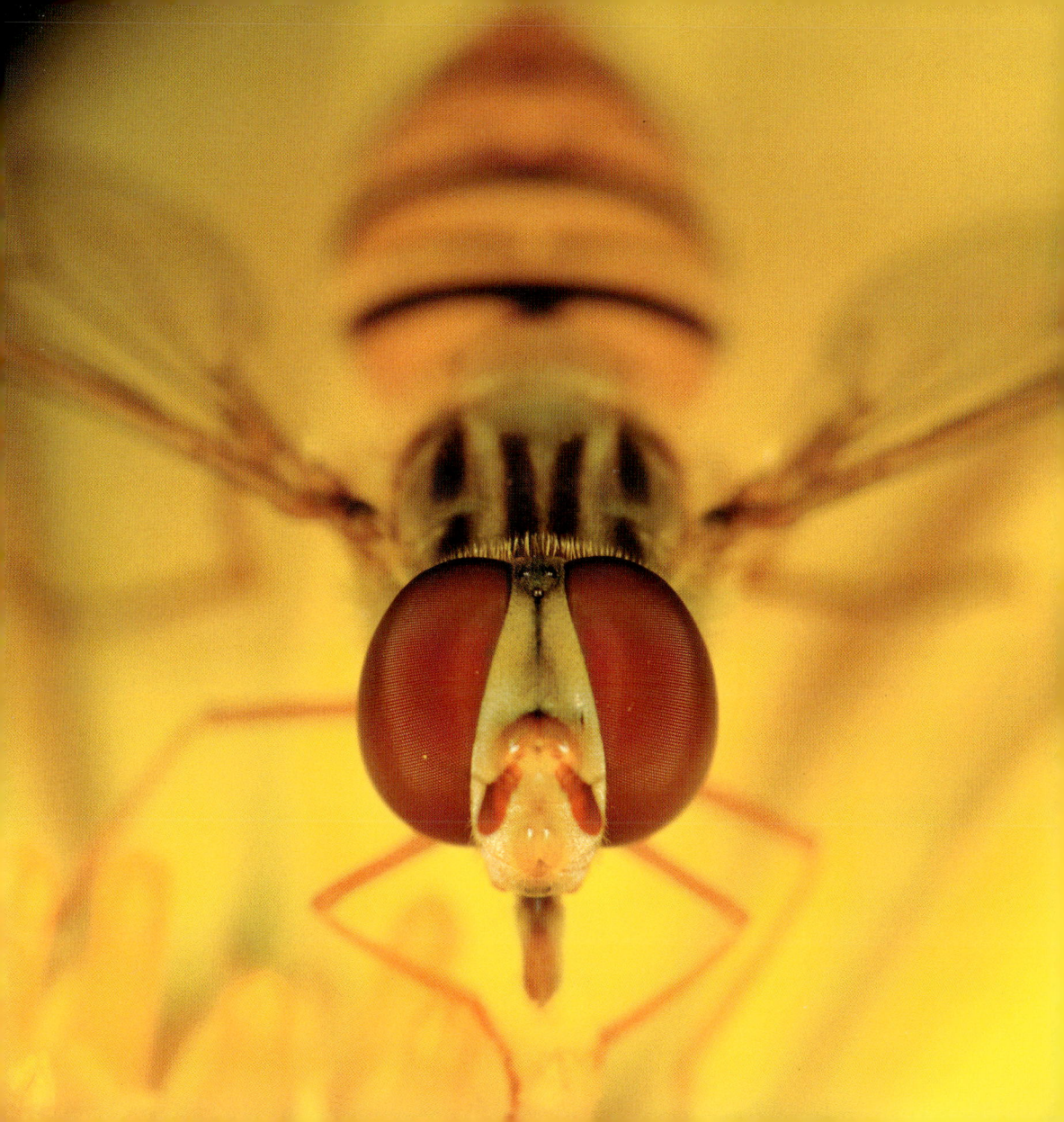

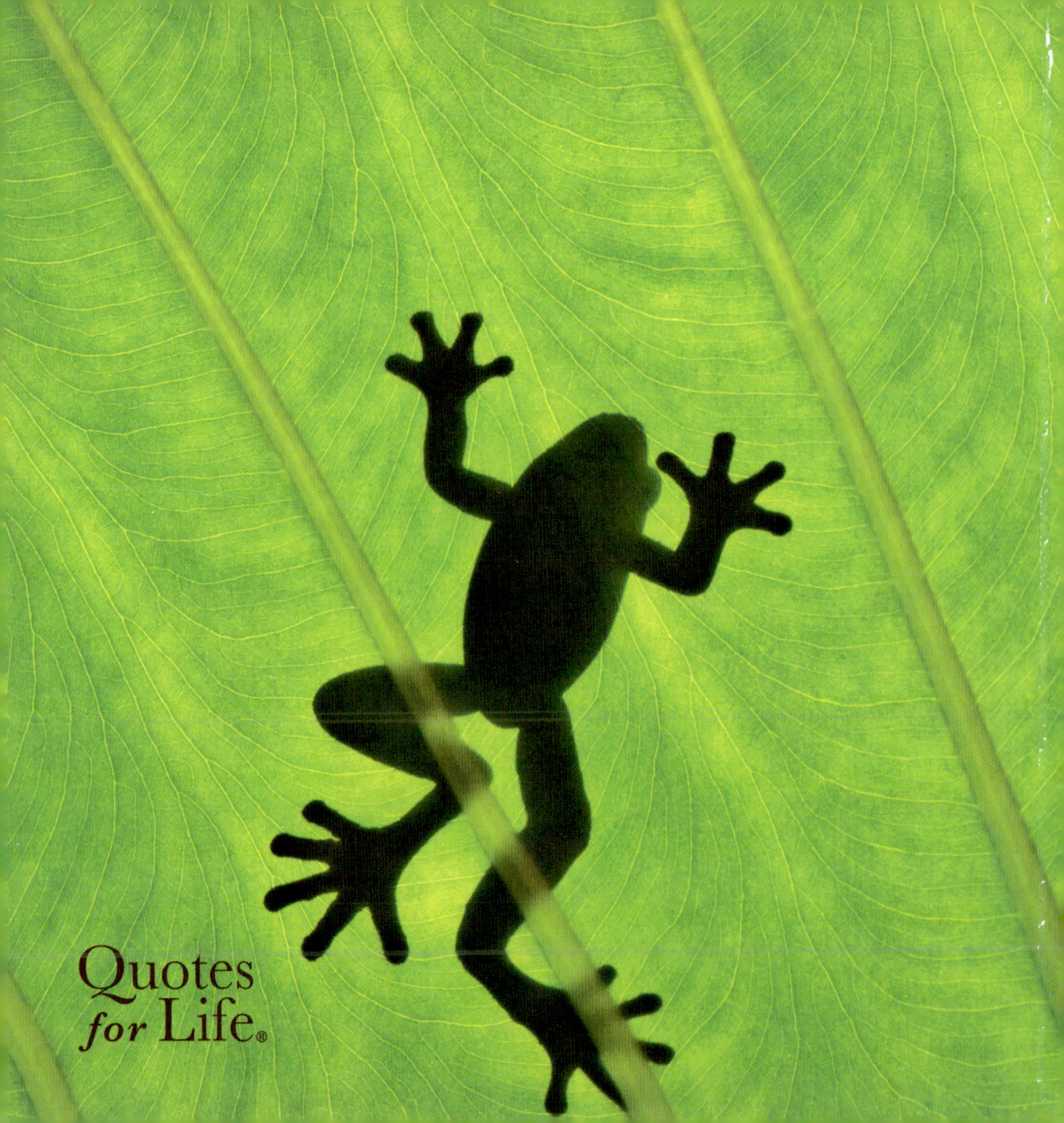

Quotes
for Life®